Marcus Garvey and the Back to Africa Movement

Lucent Library of Black History

Stuart A. Kallen

LUCENT BOOKS

An imprint of Thomson Gale, a part of The Thomson Corporation

THOMSON

GALE

Detroit • New York • San Francisco • San Diego • New Haven, Conn.
Waterville, Maine • London • Munich

LIBRARY OF CONGRESS CATALOGING-IN-PUBLICATION DATA

Kallen, Stuart A., 1955–
    Marcus Garvey and the Back to Africa Movement / by Stuart A. Kallen.
        p. cm. — (Lucent library of Black history)
    Includes bibliographical references and index.
ISBN 1-59018-838-1 (hard cover : alk. paper) 1. Garvey, Marcus, 1887-1940—Juvenile literature. 2. African Americans—Biography—Juvenile literature. 3. Jamaican Americans—Biography—Juvenile literature. 4. Civil rights workers—United States—Biography—Juvenile literature. 5. Intellectuals—United States—Biography—Juvenile literature. 6. Universal Negro Improvement Association—Juvenile literature. 7. African Americans—Civil rights—History—20th century—Juvenile literature. I. Title. II. Series.
E185.97.G3K35 2006
305.896'0730092—dc22

                                                                                        2005027286

Contents

Foreword

It has been more than five hundred years since Africans were first brought to the New World in shackles, and over 140 years since slavery was formally abolished in the United States. Over 50 years have passed since the fallacy of "separate but equal" was obliterated in the American courts, and some forty years since the watershed Civil Rights Act of 1965 guaranteed the rights and liberties of all Americans, especially those of color. Over time, these changes have become celebrated landmarks in American history. In the twenty-first century, African American men and women are politicians, judges, diplomats, professors, deans, doctors, artists, athletes, business owners, and home owners. For many, the scars of the past have melted away in the opportunities that have been found in contemporary society. Observers such as Peter N. Kirsanow, who sits on the U.S. Commission of Civil Rights, point to these accomplishments and conclude, "The growing black middle class may be viewed as proof that most of the civil rights battles have been won."

In spite of these legal victories, however, prejudice and inequality have persisted in American society. In 2003, African Americans comprised just 12 percent of the nation's population, yet accounted for 44 percent of its prison inmates and 24 percent of its poor. Racially motivated hate crimes continue to appear on the pages of major newspapers in many American cities. Furthermore, many African Americans still experience either overt or muted racism in their daily lives. A 1996 study undertaken by Professor Nancy Krieger of the Harvard School of Public Health, for example, found that 80 percent of the African American participants reported having experienced racial discrimination in one or more settings, including at work or school, applying for housing and medical care, from the police or in the courts, and on the street or in a public setting.

It is for these reasons that many believe the struggle for racial equality and justice is far from over. These episodes of discrimination threaten to shatter the illusion that America has completely overcome its racist past, causing many black Americans to become increasingly frustrated and confused. Scholar and writer Ellis Cose has described this splintered state in the following way: "I have done everything I was supposed to do. I have stayed out of trouble with the law, gone to the right schools, and worked myself nearly to death. What more do they want? Why in God's name won't they accept me as a full human being?" For Cose and others, the struggle for equality and justice has yet to be fully achieved.

In many subtle yet important ways the traumatic experiences of slavery and segregation continue to inform the way race is discussed and experienced in the twenty-first century. Indeed, it is possible that America will always grapple with the fallout from its distressing past. Ulric Haynes, dean of the Hofstra University School of Business has said, "Perhaps race will always matter, given the historical circumstances under which we came to this country." But studying this past and understanding how it contributes to present-day dialogues about race and history in America is a critical component of contemporary education. To this end, the Lucent Library of Black History offers a thorough look at the experiences that have shaped the black community and the American people as a whole. Annotated bibliographies provide readers with ideas for further research, while fully documented primary and secondary source quotations enhance the text. Each book in the series explores a different episode of black history; together they provide students with a wealth of information as well as launching points for further study and discussion.

A Controversial Man Leads a Controversial Movement

In the early decades of the twentieth century, African Americans across the United States struggled to overcome crushing racism, segregation, and institutional violence at the hands of white-majority society. Although slavery had been legally banned in 1865, the majority of black people in the United States continued to live in dire poverty. The situation for black people in the Caribbean was similar; there too, since the sixteenth century, the colonial governments of Great Britain, France, Spain, and other European countries had been exploiting the labor of imported black workers and providing little in return. It was into this world that Marcus Moziah Garvey Jr. was born in St. Ann's Bay, Jamaica, on August 17, 1887.

As a black Jamaican, Garvey experienced little prejudice firsthand but witnessed it in the extreme everywhere, elsewhere writing in 1915, "I have given my time to the study of the condition of the Negro, here, there, and everywhere, and I have come to realize that he is still the object of degradation and pity the world over, in the sense that he has no status socially, nationally, or commercially."[1]

Garvey was an educated and intelligent man who decided to devote his energies to improving the lives of black people throughout the world. To that end he founded the Universal Negro Improvement Association (UNIA) in Jamaica in 1914. Three years later he moved himself and his organization to Harlem, the bustling black neighborhood of New York City. Over the next decade, Garvey became the preeminent symbol of the controversial black nationalist and black liberation movements, attracting supporters in the millions.

Back to Africa

Garvey preached the message of the movement known as Pan-Africanism, known primarily as the "Back to Africa" movement. Based on the belief that black people would never receive fair and equal treatment in the United States, Pan-Africanists wanted to found their own nation in Africa, leaving behind the white society that had treated them so badly for so long.

However, Garvey's radical brand of racial nationalism was considered a dangerous threat by many whites who feared that black unity and black empowerment would lead to violent uprising and anarchy at home rather than mass immigration to Africa. Some equated the movement with socialism or Bolshevism (Soviet communism), which advocated the worldwide uprising of the working class and which, at the time, attracted many followers in the United States. Others opposed Pan-Africanism simply because it threatened America's racist political and cultural status quo.

Garvey's message also alienated black civil rights leaders who worked for integration and equal rights for all within American society. He was scorned, for example, by mainstream civil rights organizations such as the National Association for the Advancement of Colored People (NAACP), which argued that Garvey's movement harmed the cause of black equality. White racists, some argued, would be only too happy to forcefully rid the United States of African Americans, most of whom actually had no interest in moving around the world and starting their lives over

A button with a picture of the great Black Nationalist Marcus Garvey which declares him "Provisional President of Africa."

in Africa. Moreover, some civil rights leaders feared that Garvey's radicalism would only give the U.S. government a pretext to investigate and crack down on the activities of all black organizations, likewise setting back the cause of black civil rights.

Through his UNIA projects and his prolific published works, Garvey generated both intense hatred and intense admiration. To his followers, he was the new black Moses who would lead them to the promised land. To detractors such as William Edward Burghardt (W.E.B.) Du Bois, director of publications and research at the NAACP and perhaps the most highly respected civil rights leader of the day, Garvey was a "supreme Jamaican jackass."[2]

Such controversy made Garvey among the most famous black men of his day. He used his notoriety to promote the UNIA as the leader of a powerful black liberation movement. Preaching a message of black self-reliance, Garvey raised millions of dollars that the UNIA used to finance black-owned businesses and factories and increase black employment in Harlem and elsewhere.

Not surprisingly, Garvey's message and activities did attract the attention of powerful agencies within the U.S. government. Federal investigations into his affairs uncovered questionable, and eventually fraudulent, business practices that resulted in Garvey's imprisonment in 1925 and deportation back to his native Jamaica in 1927. Garvey's fall was as precipitous as his rise.

A Message That Resonates

Although the UNIA ultimately failed in its mission and faded from the public eye, during the years of Garvey's tenure the organization had an estimated 100,000 to 2 million members in the United States, Europe, Africa, Central and South America, and the Caribbean. In the modern civil rights movement of the 1960s, Garvey was remembered as an important link in black Americans' long struggle for freedom.

Although others before and after Garvey have espoused the Pan-African message, few expressed it as eloquently or promoted it as successfully as he did. With the oratorical skills of a preacher and the literary talent that placed him among the best writers of his day, Garvey's voice was impossible to ignore. More important, he was able to persuade thousands to join his organization and pledge to follow him where he led, even if that meant abandoning the United States for Africa. Although he was a controversial and divisive figure for his time, his vision of black pride, economic independence, and liberation are now part of mainstream African American culture. His career as a leader was short, but these elements of Garvey's message continue to resonate in the struggle for African American rights to the present day.

Chapter One

Racial Oppression and Violence in Jim Crow America

When Marcus Garvey founded the Harlem division of the Universal Negro Improvement Association in 1917, the nearly 10 million African Americans living in the United States were facing what historian Leon Litwack describes in *Trouble in Mind: Black Southerners in the Age of Jim Crow* as "the most violent and repressive period in the history of race relations in the United States."[3]

Across the nation African Americans were denied decent housing, schools, and jobs. Segregationist laws prohibited or severely restricted African Americans from voting and from using train cars, restrooms, schools, parks, theaters, restaurants, and other public facilities reserved for whites. Discriminatory laws and practices, known altogether as Jim Crow laws, enforced this racist social order. (This label originated in the 1800s, when white minstrel performers painted their faces black and sang a popular song called "Jump, Jim Crow.")

Jim Crow laws also limited blacks' ability to run for political office. Although about half a million African Americans voted, mostly in northern states, they had virtually no influence among white legislators who controlled U.S. politics. In southern states, the powerlessness of black citizens was reinforced by the practice of lynching, used to subordinate and terrorize African Americans, targeting in particular anyone who dared to challenge the entrenched social order.

Discrimination from the White House

Racism and segregation were the rule from tiny southern towns to the highest offices in the land. In 1912 Democrat Woodrow Wilson was elected president; though at least one hundred thousand black votes contributed to his victory, Wilson showed a shocking indifference to his black supporters. When he took office in January 1913, days after the fiftieth anniversary celebration of the Emancipation Proclamation that freed the slaves, Wilson reversed a fifty-year tradition of integration in federal government offices. Wilson ordered segregated toilets, lunchrooms, and work areas for those few blacks who worked at civil service jobs in Washington,

President Woodrow Wilson (pictured) disappointed thousands of black voters who had helped put him in office.

Robed members of the Ku Klux Klan march in Washington, D.C., in 1926.

D.C. This policy was followed by the transfer of black federal employees to governmental departments that were slated for dissolution. When noted black educator Booker T. Washington visited the capital, he wrote, "I have never seen the colored people so discouraged and bitter as they are at the present time."[4]

Hate Groups and Lynch Mobs

Even as Wilson was instituting segregationist measures against black workers, the vigilante group Ku Klux Klan (KKK) was reborn in Stone Mountain, Georgia. The KKK was first established by former members of the Confederate army in 1866, the year after the Civil War ended. Members of the Klan, often the most prominent politicians, policemen, and businessmen in a town, rallied support by charging that white women living on isolated plantations were vulnerable to rape by their former slaves. Wearing white hoods and sheets to disguise their identities, the group often used bogus charges of rape as an excuse to torture and lynch African Americans and sometimes Jews and other white immigrants. Effectively terrorizing the South for decades, the Klan prevented African Americans from voting and attacked black businesspeople and activists without fear of prosecution.

Although the government suppressed Klan activities in the late nineteenth century, the group was reformed in 1915 by William J. Simmons, a former Methodist minister and garter salesman. After World War I ended in 1918, the Klan continued to gain power, eventually reaching a membership of 4 million by 1925. Its political power was so strong that the group elected members to state legislatures in Texas, Oklahoma, Indiana, and elsewhere.

The masked Klansman emerged as the most obvious symbol of southern racism, but African Americans actually had more to fear from average white men and women who enthusiastically participated in mob spectacles at which blacks were brutally tortured, mutilated, and lynched. While exact numbers are uncertain, it is conservatively estimated that between 1890 and 1920, two to three black southerners were hanged, burned at the stake, or murdered by other means every week.

The degradation and horror of lynching appall the modern reader, but in this era the details of lynching were reported matter-of-factly in countless newspapers throughout the South. The execution of Luther Holbert and his wife, falsely accused of murdering their white boss in Doddsville, Mississippi, in 1904, for example, was described in the *Vicksburg Evening Post*:

> When the two Negroes were captured, they were tied to trees and while the funeral pyres were being prepared they were forced to suffer the most fiendish tortures. The blacks were forced to hold out their hands while one finger at a time was chopped off. The fingers were distributed as souvenirs. The

ears of the murderers were cut off. Holbert was beaten severely, his skull was fractured and one of his eyes, knocked out with a stick. . . . The most excruciating form of punishment consisted in the use of a large corkscrew in the hands of some of the mob. This instrument was bored into the flesh of the man and woman, in the arms, legs and body, and then pulled out.[5]

The article fails to question the Holberts' guilt or innocence. In fact, Mr. Holbert was seized simply because he had had an argument with his white boss, who refused to pay him. Also ignored was the fact that another black couple mistaken for the Holberts had already received the same treatment that day. Lynching, however, was not about justice. It was a way to keep the black community terrorized and fearful of speaking out for their rights. As one unnamed black man who observed a lynching noted, "One Negro swinging from a tree will serve as well as another to terrorize the community."[6]

During most lynchings, the tormentors did not hide their identities with masks like those worn by the KKK. None feared being arrested for their actions and, in fact, participants often included sheriff's deputies, mayors, politicians, judges, and other local government officials.

Lynching also generated a circuslike atmosphere that attracted spectators by the hundreds from surrounding areas. Postcards of lynchings were even printed as souvenirs. They showed smiling young children hoisted on their father's shoulders to see the event while women, wearing their best clothes, held babies in their arms. At a 1909 lynching in Rankin County, Mississippi, the local newspaper reported that three thousand people had witnessed the execution, and added, "Some ladies were present. . . . A few were nursing infants who tugged at the mother's breasts, while the mother kept her eyes on the gallows. She didn't want to lose any part of the program she had come miles to see, and to tell the neighbors back home."[7] It was also reported that onlookers removed victims' organs, teeth, bones, and other body parts and later sold them for ten or twenty-five cents to those who could not attend. One such grisly souvenir, the charred knuckles of a lynching victim in Georgia, were prominently displayed in the front window of an Atlanta grocery store in 1899.

The Great Migration North

Lynching was but one of the miseries endured by black southerners. They were an oppressed minority by every social measure. Ninety percent of African Americans in the United States lived in the South in 1910; they were the poorest and least educated people in the country. They suffered the highest rates of ill health, malnutrition, and infant mortality. In addition, as one

"Behind the Veil"

In the first decades of the twentieth century, black Americans were terrorized by the Ku Klux Klan and were discriminated against politically, socially, and economically. Under such harsh conditions, African American culture developed largely apart from white society, as Leon Litwack explains in *Trouble in Mind: Black Southerners in the Age of Jim Crow:*

> Under severe constraints, black Southerners created a world of their own "behind the veil," as [NAACP founder] W.E.B. Du Bois described it, and found ways to respond to their situation. . . . It may be found in the families black Southerners maintained, in the institutions they created, in the schools they worked so hard to sustain, in the businesses they established, in the churches they attended, and in the voluntary associations that afforded them important outlets and support. This interior life, largely unknown and incomprehensible to whites, permitted black Southerners to survive and endure.
>
> Denied access to the political process, limited in what they could acquire in the schools, and dehumanized in popular culture, black Southerners were compelled to find other ways to express their deepest feelings and to demonstrate their individual and collective integrity. What helped to sustain them through bondage and a tortured freedom had been a rich oral expressive tradition, consisting of folk beliefs, proverbs, humor, sermons, spirituals, gospel songs, hollers, work songs, the blues, and jazz. Through a variety of expression, black men and women conveyed not only their disillusionment, alienation, and frustration, but also their joys, aspirations, triumphs, and expectations; they used such expression both to confront their situation and to overcome and transcend it.

black woman in Alabama said, "There was a feeling of unrest, insecurity, almost panic. . . . Where can we go to feel that security which other people feel?"[8]

For many, the answer was to move to the industrial centers of the North, such as Cleveland, Detroit, Chicago, and New York. What began as a trickle of about 7,000 in 1897 turned into a wave later known as the great migration. Between 1916 and 1918 alone, nearly 2 million southern African Americans moved to the North, and in the decade that followed, another million made the journey.

The peak of the great migration occurred while World War I was ravaging Europe, from 1914 to 1918. This global conflict played a major role in the population shift: In 1915 the U.S. government cut off virtually all European immigration, which caused a severe labor shortage in the North. When the United States entered the war in 1917, tens of thousands of white northern factory workers were drafted into the military. At the same time, the industrial capacity of the nation was rapidly expanding to meet wartime manufacturing and supply needs. This situation provided unprecedented job opportunities for African Americans too old for military service. In the South, the average wage for an unskilled black laborer was forty to seventy-five cents a day. In a northern factory, the same worker could earn from three to eight dollars a day. Although the cost of liv-

Gospel singers, such as Thomas Dorsey and his all female quartet, sustained African Americans through bondage and a tortured freedom.

ing was much higher in the North, the high wages were an irresistible incentive to southerners looking for a better life.

In 1915 the biggest cities, notably Chicago and New York, already had thriving segregated black communities. African Americans who were northern natives had spent decades nurturing black civic institutions, newspapers, businesses, social agencies, and political organizations. The great influx of rural southern blacks, while good for African Americans in many ways, put great pressure on these institutions. In *Black Chicago: The Making of a Negro Ghetto, 1890–1920*, historian Allan H. Spear describes the new problems in Chicago, the city with the nation's second-largest black population:

> As the migration progressed, Negro leaders became increasingly aware of the problems presented by the newcomers. The crude, rustic ways of many of the migrants, their inability to maintain accepted standards of cleanliness, and their traditionally sycophantic [overly humble] demeanor in the presence of whites antagonized the old settlers. Not only did the more established Negroes find the newcomers' habits personally offensive but they felt that they diminished the status of all Negroes in the eyes of the white community. The old settlers began to formulate a myth that became an article of faith in later years. Discrimination, they argued, was minimal before the migration and it was the behavior of the newcomers that induced it.[9]

Despite the cultural clash, African American churches and organizations such as the Urban League instituted social programs to help the new arrivals find jobs, living quarters, and other necessities.

The World's Greatest Negro Metropolis

Such programs were acutely necessary in Harlem, where the majority of black New York residents lived. Although the neighborhood occupies less than 2 square miles (5 sq. km) of Manhattan Island in northern New York City, by the mid-1920s it was home to more than 350,000 African Americans. In addition to its native New Yorker population, Harlem was a melting pot of black

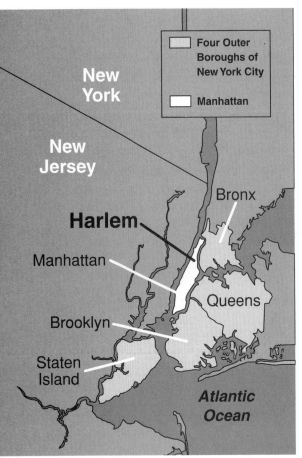

Four Outer Boroughs of New York City

Manhattan

New York

New Jersey

Bronx

Harlem

Manhattan

Queens

Brooklyn

Staten Island

Atlantic Ocean

immigrants from Jamaica, Haiti, Cuba, Puerto Rico, and Africa as well as from the southern states of Louisiana, Mississippi, Georgia, Alabama, and the Carolinas. These newcomers contributed to a unique mix of cultures, cuisine, music, languages, religions, and fashion in the neighborhood, earning Harlem the nickname of "The World's Greatest Negro Metropolis." The rise of Harlem as the center of black American culture, however, was a direct result of white racism and prejudicial real estate and banking policies.

The first influx of black residents to Harlem began at a single apartment house on 31 West 133rd Street. In 1905 this building was filled with black tenants whose monthly rent was five dollars more than that charged to their white neighbors. Around this time a black real estate agent, Philip A. Payton, organized the Afro-American Realty Company and began buying and leasing houses and apartments in Harlem specifically for occupancy by black people. Most white residents of Harlem, however, were displeased by this new development. They formed organizations that demanded that banks stop making real estate loans to blacks. The banks stopped lending, but black residency grew anyway and Harlem's racial demographics grew more and more unequal. In 1925 author and educator James Weldon Johnson described the situation in *The New Negro: An Interpretation*:

Negroes not only continued to occupy available apartment houses, but began to purchase private dwellings. . . . Then the whole movement, in the eyes of the whites, took on the aspect of an "invasion"; they became panic-stricken and began fleeing as from a plague. The presence of one colored family in a block, no matter how well bred and orderly, was sufficient to precipitate a flight. House after house and block after block was actually deserted. It was a great demonstration of human beings running amuck. None of them stopped to reason why they were doing it or what would happen if they didn't. The banks and lending companies holding mortgages on these deserted houses were compelled to take them over. For some time they held these houses vacant, preferring to do that and carry the charges than to rent or to sell them to colored people. But values dropped and continued to drop until, at the outbreak of war

A bustling East Harlem in 1922 was part of New York's vibrant African American community.

in Europe [in 1914], property in north Harlem had reached the nadir [lowest point].[10]

Whites took flight and black Harlem became more self-sufficient. Many black laborers were earning high enough wages to save and invest their money. Meanwhile, community leaders encouraged neighborhood residents to buy houses and apartments. For example, when the Metropolitan Baptist Church bought a beautiful brownstone church building on Seventh Avenue, Reverend W.W. Brown urged his congregation to buy property during his weekly sermons. Many took his advice. This trend created some of the first black real estate moguls in New York history.

The Harlem Renaissance

Between 1919 and 1929 the expansion of homeownership in Harlem coincided with an era of unprecedented creativity in African American literature, music, dance, and fine arts. Called the New Negro Renaissance by some and the Harlem Renaissance by others, this whirlwind of creativity was unmatched anywhere else in the United States. The renaissance influenced American culture in general while enriching African American society. Never before

A Variety of Terms

During the 1920s the terms commonly used to refer to African Americans were a matter of some controversy. *Negro, black,* and *colored* were all accepted terms in polite white society. Black civil rights activists and entities such as the *Chicago Defender* newspaper often coined new terms—*Aframericans, Afro-Americans, race man,* even *Ethiopian,* for example—to distance African Americans from derogatory connotations of old terms or to emphasize the African roots of black Americans. Marcus Garvey favored the term *Negro,* but many of his contemporaries considered this word patronizing and demeaning and objected to its use in favor of terms that emphasized blacks' equal status.

had so many white Americans embraced the books, music, artwork, expressions, and fashion sense of African Americans.

The renaissance was led by what author Alain Locke called "the new Negro."[11] Harlem quickly became a magnet for talented black dancers, singers, painters, playwrights, actors, and musicians as well as businesspeople and tourists from across the globe. As Johnson noted, "Harlem is indeed the great Mecca for the sight-seer; the pleasure-seeker, the curious, the adventurous, the enterprising, the ambitious and the talented of the whole Negro world; for the lure of it has reached down to every island of the [Caribbean] Sea and has penetrated even into Africa."[12]

The good times were part of the decade called the Roaring Twenties, so named because the postwar American economy was growing at its fastest rate in history, the stock market was minting new millionaires nearly every day, and modernism was taking hold in all sectors of society. At the same time, conservative trends in American culture were manifested primarily as Prohibition, the ban on the sale and manufacture of alcoholic beverages. Virtually overnight, hundreds of nightclubs and cabarets that illegally sold alcohol, called speakeasies, opened in Harlem. In these places, fashionable, well-to-do white patrons listened to jazz and blues written and performed by black musicians. Plays, revues, and theatrical productions with all-black casts were packing in white audiences, who largely supported segregation outside of their entertainment habits.

The Harlem Hellfighters

Many had marked the beginning of the Harlem Renaissance of the 1920s as February 17, 1919. On that day thirteen hundred veterans of the all-black 369th Infantry Regiment marched up Fifth Avenue. The infantry, known as the Harlem Hellfighters, consisted of the first black troops sent to fight on the European battlefront in World War I. Their bravery in battle was legendary on both sides of the Atlantic Ocean, and their exposure to very different standards of racial equality in Europe permanently changed their attitudes about, and reduced their tolerance for, American racism.

The soldiers drew polite applause from white citizens, including New York governor Al Smith, as they marched down Fifth

Avenue. But after crossing over to Lenox and passing 130th Street, the soldiers entered Harlem, and the cheers became a hero's welcome. As the *New York Age* newspaper wrote, "Hellfighters marched between two howling walls of humanity."[13]

Leading the march were the sixty members of the Hellfighters' military band, led by James Reese Europe. As the band broke into a jazzy version of "Here Comes My Daddy," girlfriends and relatives joined the ranks of soldiers. Tenants on rooftops tossed a torrent of pennants, flags, banners, and scarves on the heroes.

When that band turned the corner to enter Harlem, the black community turned another corner. The new heroes of Harlem returned with new fashions, new dignity, and new expectations. After fighting in World War I, being celebrated in Europe and decorated in France, Harlem's black veterans were not content to quietly accept traditional prejudice. To combat the twin challenges of racism and urban poverty, these black veterans were eager to fight for equal rights at home.

At the same time, however, there was no clear leader who could organize the powerful wave of discontent building in

Members of the all-black 369th Infantry Regiment proudly march in a parade in New York City in 1919.

Diverse Elements of Negro Life

In the 1910s Harlem became a melting pot of black cultures from across the globe. In his 1925 book, *The New Negro: An Interpretation*, Alain Locke explains the origins of the new residents and their motives for moving to Harlem:

> Here in Manhattan is not merely the largest Negro community in the world, but the first concentration in history of so many diverse elements of Negro life. It has attracted the African, the West Indian, the Negro American; has brought together the Negro of the North and the Negro of the South; the man from the city and the man from the town and village; the peasant, the student, the business man, the professional man, artist, poet, musician, adventurer and worker, preacher and criminal, exploiter and social outcast. Each group has come with its own separate motives and for its own special ends, but their greatest experience has been the finding of one another. [Exclusion] and prejudice have thrown these dissimilar elements into a common area of contact and interaction. Within this area, race sympathy and unity have determined a further fusing of sentiment and experience. So what began in terms of segregation becomes more and more, as its elements mix and react, the laboratory of a great race-welding. . . . In Harlem, Negro life is seizing upon its first chances for group expression and self-determination. It is—or promises at least to be—a race capital.

African American society. This feeling was encapsulated in an editorial called "A Moses Needed" in the *Washington Bee* newspaper: "The colored race is greatly in need of a Moses . . . a man of the people and designated by the people."[14]

Even as the editorial appeared, a Jamaican immigrant named Marcus Garvey was settling into life in Harlem. Within a year he would become the new black Moses, and his leadership would galvanize a new era of black activism.

Chapter Two

A New Black Moses

Before 1917 what little organized black civil rights activity there was in the United States was sponsored by a few groups, notably the National Association for the Advancement of Colored People (NAACP), founded in 1910. A few well-respected but aging leaders, including Booker T. Washington and W.E.B. Du Bois, had achieved national prominence, but there was a general dearth of leadership in the African American community, especially on the local level, and the overall status of southern blacks seemed to be worsening. In 1917 Marcus Garvey stepped into this leadership vacuum.

Unlike African Americans, Garvey was not exposed to bigotry at an early age. Born into the mixed-race society of Jamaica in 1887, he attended integrated schools and knew little about overt racial hatred. In fact, Garvey once wrote that he first heard the term *Negro* and the racial slur *nigger* when he was fourteen years old. At the age of eighteen, as Garvey became aware of subtle class distinctions in Jamaica based on race, he set out to see more of the world and was exposed to harsh racial discrimination for the first time.

During the young man's travels through South and Central America he saw black laborers on sugarcane and banana plantations treated little better than slaves. Throughout Ecuador, Nicaragua, Honduras, Colombia, and Venezuela, Garvey saw blacks experiencing great hardship and suffering from the effects of discrimination and prejudice. These encounters provoked Garvey's indignation: "I asked, 'Where is the black man's Government?' 'Where is his King and his kingdom?' 'Where is his President, his country, his ambassador, his army, his navy, his men of big affairs?' I could not find them, and then I declared, 'I will help to make them.'"[15]

Launching the UNIA

Garvey spent about eighteen months traveling in Europe between 1912 and 1914, earning money sporadically by writing articles and giving speeches. During this period his ideas about helping the black race took shape. Returning to Jamaica aboard ship in July 1914, the twenty-six-year-old Garvey sat in his bunk and jotted down the objectives of a new organization and a startling new destination:

> To establish a Universal Confraternity [association] among the race; to promote the spirit of pride and love; to reclaim the fallen; to administer to and assist the needy; to assist in civilizing the backward tribes of Africa; to assist in the development of Independent Negro nations and communities; to

Educator Booker T. Washington had gained respect and prominence as a civil rights leader among African Americans.

25

W.E.B. Du Bois was a noted scholar and educator, and a founding member of the NAACP.

establish a central nation for the race [in Africa], where they will be given the opportunity to develop themselves; to establish Commissaries and Agencies in the principle countries and cities of the world for the representation of all Negroes; to promote a conscientious Spiritual worship among the native tribes of Africa; to establish Universities, Colleges, Academies and Schools for racial education and culture of the people; to improve the general conditions of Negroes everywhere.[16]

Garvey returned to Jamaica on July 15, 1914, and promptly set himself to the task of black liberation. Within five days he founded the Universal Negro Improvement Association and African Communities League (UNIA and ACL). His goal, he wrote nine years later, was to advance a program "uniting all the negro peoples of the world into one great body to establish a country and Government absolutely their own."[17]

Before long, however, Garvey's grand vision collided with the reality of Jamaican society. First, it antagonized black Jamaicans. People of African descent made up about 90 percent of the island's inhabitants, and they did not face the kind of discrimination that African Americans faced. More important, they did not identify themselves as Negroes—they considered the term an insult and were not supportive when Garvey used it. White Jamaicans hardly found Garvey's ideas any more appealing. Garvey's second wife, author Amy Jacques Garvey, explains: "The word 'Negro' created opposition and prevented help from 'better-off colored people,' who felt that Negro was synonymous with low, good-for-nothing. To the . . . whites it suggested an organized black majority, which they felt would be dangerous to their economic overlordship."[18]

Garvey was also forced to confront black-on-black racism: In Jamaica's multiracial society, social class was determined to some degree by shades of skin color. Because of his dark skin, Garvey writes, "I was a black man and therefore had no right to lead; in the opinion of the 'colored' element, leadership should only have been in the hands of a yellow or very light man. On such flimsy prejudices our race has been [held back]."[19]

Soapbox Speeches

Garvey struggled in Jamaica, opposed both by indifferent blacks and white landowners, corporations, and newspapers. His only encouragement came from his correspondence with Booker T. Washington, founder of the Tuskegee Institute in Alabama and a champion of black education. Garvey decided to travel to the United States, meet the famous Washington, and set up his own schools. He also planned to establish American branches of the UNIA in major cities.

By the time Garvey arrived in the United States in March 1916, however, Washington had died. Undeterred, Garvey decided to go on a speaking tour of the United States and visited thirty-eight

Marcus Garvey: Printer, Editor, Writer

Marcus Garvey was trained as a printer when he was fourteen years old. With this background, Garvey was experienced in newspaper production and decided to publish his first newspaper, the *Watchman*, in 1910. The paper folded after three issues, and Garvey decided to leave Jamaica because, in his own words, "the politics of my country so disgusted me that I started to travel." While traveling through South and Central America, Garvey observed the squalid working conditions for blacks on large plantations.

During his travels, Garvey worked as an editor of *La Nación* and the *Bluefields Messenger* in Costa Rica and *La Prensa* in Panama. He used these forums to editorialize about the plight of black workers. After returning to Jamaica, Garvey continued to write articles about colonialism and racism. In 1913 his article "British West Indies in the Mirror of Civilization: History Making by Colonial Negroes" was published in both the *African Times* and in *Orient Review* magazine. In June 1914 his article "The Evolution of Latter-day Slaves: Jamaica, a Country of Black and White" was published in the *Tourist*.

Marcus Garvey wrote many articles about colonialism and racism.

Garvey was a prolific writer until his death, and his collected works provide detailed accounts of his life, the Universal Negro Improvement Association, and a historical record of black life in the United States, England, and Jamaica.

states over the following year. During his travels, Garvey experienced American racism for the first time, witnessing a society built on black disenfranchisement and poverty, Jim Crow laws, and the terrorism of lynching.

More determined than ever to unite African Americans, Africans, and West Indians into a powerful political force, Garvey returned to New York in 1917. He took his message to the streets, preaching to passersby while perched atop a wooden soapbox. He was mostly broke, and he later said that on several occasions he fell off his soapbox, dizzy from hunger. During these hard times, walking the streets of Harlem with holes in his shoes, Garvey developed his romanticized vision of founding a nation in the tropical paradise of Africa. Although he had never visited the continent, he hoped to lead his people there someday, as Jacques Garvey writes: "Africa to him was like his birthplace; he loved the profusion of tropical growth; he loved the people who lived near nature. Africa! Nearly twelve million square miles [31 million sq. km] of it! What a wonderful gift from God! If only he could get his people to appreciate it the way he did. . . . He must!"[20]

"Outrages Against Mankind"

Garvey settled in Harlem in the summer of 1917 amid a general atmosphere of national crisis. The United States had entered World War I on April 6, and by the end of the year 370,000 African Americans would be serving in the military, mostly in segregated units.

The bitter fighting in Europe had a civil rights counterpart in the United States. In East St. Louis, Illinois, one of the bloodiest race riots in the nation's history took place between July 1 and July 3. The riot began after local factories began hiring African Americans who had recently migrated from the South. A white mob, fearful of a southern black "invasion," began burning homes in the city's African American neighborhood, intending to destroy the entire community. Police stood by and watched as nearly two hundred black people were shot, beaten, or burned to death and 250 buildings were destroyed. After the flames died down, six thousand were left homeless. The riot received widespread coverage in the press and quickly became a symbol of African American suffering at the hands of white mobs.

At this time Garvey tailored a message to address concerns about racial violence and the war. In a speech before a large, enthusiastic New York crowd assembled in Lafayette Hall on July 8, Garvey stated:

> The East St. Louis Riot, or rather massacre . . . will go down in history as one of the bloodiest outrages against mankind for which any class of people could be held guilty. . . . I do not know what special meaning the people who slaughtered the Negroes of East St. Louis have for democracy of which they are the custodians, but I do know that it has no literal meaning for me as used and applied by these same lawless people. America, that has been ringing the bells of the world, proclaiming to the nations and the peoples . . . that she has democracy to give to all and sundry . . . has herself no satisfaction to give 12,000,000 of her own [black] citizens. . . . With all the service that the Negro gave he is still a despised creature in the eye of the white people, for if he were not despised, the 90,000,000 whites in this country would never allow such outrages as the East St. Louis massacre.[21]

Garvey's stirring speech earned him the attention he had been seeking for so long. As a speaker who could rouse the emotions of his audience, Garvey was quickly recognized as a bona fide black leader. He decided to seize the moment and establish the first U.S. branch of the UNIA.

"A Friendly and Constructive Hand"

Throughout the summer and fall, the ambitious Garvey built a following by giving weekly Sunday lectures to hundreds of people at Lafayette Hall. In January 1918 he opened the first official meeting of the New York branch of the UNIA. This initial gathering attracted only thirteen members, who duly elected Garvey president. The UNIA continued to attract new members, however, and on July 2, 1918, the association was incorporated as a social service organization under New York law. The purpose of the UNIA, according to the certificate of incorporation, was "to promote and practice the principles of Benevolence, and . . . to extend a friendly and constructive hand to the Negroes of the United States."[22]

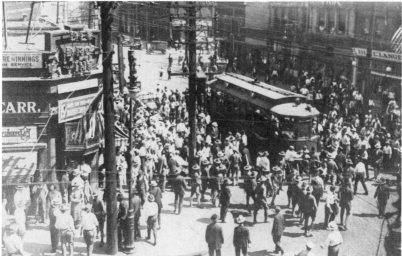

East St. Louis burned with hatred and frustration in 1917. A devastated neighborhood (top) and a white mob's attack on a black man (bottom) present lasting images of the race riot.

The official papers of the UNIA suggest that Garvey must have spent a great deal of his time formulating the group's bylaws. The UNIA's *Constitution and Book of Law* includes page after page fancifully detailing the duties of dozens of (as yet unrecruited) officers. Garvey also took the time to write poetic hymns for opening and closing meetings and even a national anthem about the glories of Africa.

On July 31, 1918, Garvey separately incorporated the African Communities League (ACL). He believed that black independence could be realized through the ACL, and had great plans for

The Preamble to the UNIA Constitution

When Marcus Garvey formed the Universal Negro Improvement Association, he wrote a dramatic statement to serve as the constitution for the organization. It is reprinted in *Garvey and Garveyism* by Amy Jacques Garvey:

> The Universal Negro Improvement Association and African Communities' League is a social, friendly, humanitarian, charitable, educational, institutional, constructive, and expansive Society, and is founded by persons desiring to the utmost, to work for the general uplift of the Negro peoples of the world. And the members pledge themselves to do all in their power to conserve the rights of their noble race, and to respect the rights of all mankind, believing always in the Brotherhood of Man and the Fatherhood of God. The motto of the Organization is: One God! One Aim! One Destiny! Therefore, let justice be done to all mankind, realizing that if the strong oppresses the weak, confusion and discontent will ever mark the path of man, but with love, faith and charity towards all, the reign of peace and plenty will be heralded into the world and the generations of men shall be called Blessed.

Marcus Garvey addresses members of the Universal Negro Improvement Association.

the corporation. It was set up to establish its own manufacturing facilities and retail outlets that would produce and sell all manner of food, glassware, appliances, and other useful goods. The ACL was also incorporated to manage independently owned real estate companies, restaurants, bakeries, publishing companies, and stores. To finance ACL operations, Garvey planned to sell thousands of shares of stock to investors. He also embarked on a national speaking tour to raise money for the company.

In the late summer of 1918 Garvey began writing, editing, and publishing the official UNIA newspaper, the *Negro World*, a venture that also fell under the ACL umbrella. The paper, first published August 3, was distributed free by volunteers, often pushed under the doors of people's apartments in the hours before dawn. The *Negro World* was an effective forum for Garvey's ideas and philosophy, and membership in the UNIA began to increase sharply. When Garvey gave a speech on November 11, 1918, to celebrate the armistice ending World War I, more than five thousand people attended.

"Africa for Africans"

Garvey's fame, along with UNIA membership, continued to grow. As Imanuel Geiss writes in *The Pan-African Movement: A History of Pan-Africanism in America, Europe, and Africa*, "Thanks to his magnificent eloquence, organizational talents and wealth of ideas, Garvey was able within a few months to expand the UNIA's influence beyond Harlem and to build up associations in the large industrial cities of the North into which Afro-American [labor] had been pouring during the wartime boom."[23]

Membership estimates vary, but Garvey claimed that the organization swelled from six hundred to twelve thousand members in "the space of a couple of months."[24] Part of this growth may be attributed to the ease with which a person could join the UNIA. With thirty-five cents, a photograph, and the willingness to pledge his or her support for the association, any person of African descent was eligible to join. Garvey was able to sign up thousands of cooks, maids, workmen, and others who were eager to join a group that gave them a sense of racial pride and community and the promise of jobs.

By this time, more than fifty thousand people were receiving the *Negro World*. The paper was the official instrument spreading Garvey's message of black nationalism, unity, independence, and pride in African heritage. Its circulation success stimulated interest in new chapters of the UNIA, and by early 1919 the group officially boasted thirty local U.S. chapters and several chapters overseas. By the middle of 1919 that number, according to Garvey, had mushroomed into a total of three hundred branches with more than 2 million members. Garvey's figures were almost certainly exaggerated, however, and some critics claim that the UNIA never had more than 80,000 members.

Whatever the exact number, the UNIA was so popular in Harlem that Garvey was able to purchase a large auditorium for group meetings and rallies, which he named Liberty Hall. Nearly every evening Garvey appeared at the hall to give a speech or lecture on the issues of the day and implore black people to wrest the African continent from its European colonial governors. On many occasions his audience exceeded six thousand people.

With a reach that extended across the United States and into several foreign countries, there is little doubt that Garvey was now perceived by many as the new black Moses. Historian Roi Ottley, a scholar of black history, explains how the leader qualified for this role:

After the war, there was a resurgence of Ku Klux Klan influence; another decade of racial hatred and

A handbill announces a 1917 forthcoming speech by Marcus Garvey.

BIG MASS MEETING

A CALL TO THE
COLORED CITIZENS
OF
ATLANTA, GEORGIA
To Hear the Great West Indian Negro Leader
HON. MARCUS GARVEY
President of the Universal Negro Improvement Association of Jamaica, West Indies.

Big Bethel A. M. E. Church
Corner Auburn Avenue and Butler Street

SUNDAY AFTERNOON, AT 3 O'CLOCK
MARCH 25, 1917

He brings a message of inspiration to the 12,000,000 of our people in this country.
SUBJECT:
"The Negroes of the West Indies, after 78 years of Emancipation." With a general talk on the world position of the race.

An orator of exceptional force, Professor Garvey has spoken to packed audiences in England, New York, Boston, Washington, Philadelphia, Chicago, Milwaukee, St. Louis, Detroit, Cleveland, Cincinatti, Indianapolis, Louisville, Nashville and other cities. He has travelled to the principal countries of Europe, and was the first Negro to speak to the Veterans' Club of London, England. This is the only chance to hear a great man who has taken his message before the world. **COME OUT EARLY TO SECURE SEATS.** It is worth travelling 1,000 miles to hear.

All Invited. Rev. H. H. Singleton, D.D., Pastor.

open lawlessness had set in, and Negroes again were prominent among the victims. Meantime, administration leaders
were quite pointed in trying to persuade Negroes that in
spite of their full participation in the war effort they could
expect no change in their traditional status in America. . . .
Negroes were more than ready for a Moses—one done in
black preferably. . . . Negroes were faced with a choice
between *racialism* and *radicalism.* Marcus Garvey settled the
question for thousands by forming the Universal Negro
Improvement Association . . . and preaching with great zeal
for a pilgrimage of black men "Back to Africa." He rallied
men to the slogan, "Africa for Africans."[25]

Backlash

Though Garvey's image as the new black Moses was readily accepted by his African American audiences, the fiery agitator was considered a dangerous radical by powerful white officials. For example, in March 1919 Garvey gave a speech to cheering throngs at
Madison Square Garden in Manhattan. Galvanizing the crowd,
Garvey sounded like a revolutionary when he proclaimed, "It will
be a terrible day when the blacks draw the sword to fight for their
liberty. I call upon you [400 million] blacks to give the blood you
have shed for the white man to make Africa a republic for the
Negro."[26] In another speech, Garvey told his audience, "Get together from now on and be ready to get into Africa. . . . [We must build]
battleships and raise armies, after we get a good foothold in Africa,
which must positively be in the next twelve months."[27]

The bureau began to keep a close watch on Garvey, hiring
undercover informants to file reports on his speeches, articles in
the *Negro World,* and UNIA activities. The reports contained highly charged language, calling Garvey a Negro agitator, his newspaper Negro propaganda and referring to his speeches as sedition,
a treasonous crime that carried a long jail sentence and the
prospect of summary deportation without trial.

Garvey's rhetoric and growing influence attracted the attention
of the local authorities and agents for the Bureau of Investigation,
forerunner of the FBI. In April 1918 agent C.E. Campbell wrote a
memo to his superiors stating, "There was a man by the name Garvey (colored) who preaches every night against the white people."[28]

The bureau began to keep a close watch on Garvey, hiring
undercover informants to file reports on his speeches, articles in
the *Negro World,* and UNIA activities. The reports contained highly charged language, calling Garvey a Negro agitator, his newspaper Negro propaganda and referring to his speeches as sedition,
a treasonous crime that carried a long jail sentence and the
prospect of summary deportation without trial.

Black Pride

—■—

Garvey's ideology grew out of his observations that black people were discriminated against not because of their actions but because of their race. To Garvey, the negative concepts of the black race had to be reversed in white people's minds and in black people's attitudes. To do so, Garvey formulated a message of black pride, described by Tony Martin in *Race First:*

> For Garvey, the black man was universally oppressed on racial grounds, and any program of emancipation would have to be built around the question of race first. The race became a "political entity" which would have to be redeemed. . . .
>
> Garvey went about the task of converting the disabilities of race into a positive tool of liberation with a thorough aggressiveness. . . . [He declared:] "The world has made being black a crime, and I have felt it in common with men who suffer like me, and instead of making it a crime I hope to make it a virtue." Accordingly, the consciousness of Garvey's followers was saturated with the new doctrine. Black dolls were manufactured for black children . . . he encouraged his followers to support their black businessmen and professionals . . . he frowned upon advertisements of a racially demeaning nature. *The Negro World* sponsored beauty contests and published photographs of beautiful black women, a subject on which Garvey waxed poetic—"Black queen of beauty, thou hast given color to the world." Indeed, practically every aspect of the organization was designed to bolster the black man's self-esteem and to foster pride in self.

Even during this period of heightened anti-immigrant sentiment and suspicion of all political opinion viewed as anti-American or anarchist, Garvey stood out. The attention given to Garvey by federal agents demonstrates his importance and the extent to which his message was perceived as a threat. Within a few years he had transformed himself from a hungry soapbox preacher into a symbol of worldwide black nationalism. With unequaled ambition and few doubts about himself or his message, Garvey had become, at least by his own measure, a major force on the world stage who brought hope to millions of followers.

Chapter Three

Spreading the Pan-African Message

In August 1920 the first Universal Negro Improvement Association convention was held in New York City. During the boisterous, month-long affair, twenty-five thousand members unanimously elected Marcus Garvey the "provisional president of Africa." In this role Garvey presented himself as the leader of an African government in exile, which, according to UNIA position papers, was said to represent all black people wherever they lived in the world.

As the provisional president of Africa, Garvey bestowed grandiose titles upon his closest supporters in his New York inner circle. This new Harlem nobility included the Duke of the Nile, the Earl of Congo, the Viscount of Niger, and Baron Zambezi. The bearers of these titles took to appearing in custom-tailored military-style uniforms, designed by Garvey, that were bedecked with decorations and medals of the provisional African government.

During the convention the UNIA also adopted a national flag— a red, black, and green banner that was said to be the official flag

Uniformed black women march proudly through Harlem in a parade that preceded a UNIA convention in 1924.

of the motherland, or Africa, using the official colors of the African race. According to Garvey, the red in the flag symbolized the "color of the blood which men must shed for their redemption and liberty"; black was "the color of the noble and distinguished race to which we belong," and green stood for "the luxuriant vegetation of our Motherland."[29]

After the opening ceremony, dozens of UNIA flags were carried by the uniformed royalty in a huge parade that brought Harlem to a standstill. With thousands of delegates, the three-hour pageant stretched for ten city blocks and was described in a UNIA report as "the greatest [parade] ever staged anywhere in the world by Negroes."[30] Garvey was the central focus of the parade, seated regally in the back seat of a decorated Packard convertible. Delegates from dozens of UNIA chapters carried banners that read "Garvey the Negro Moses—Long May He Live," "Africa Must be Free," "The Negro Fought in Europe; He Can Fight in Africa," "Africa a Nation One and Indivisible," and the UNIA slogan "Africa for Africans."[31]

The Roots of Pan-Africanism

"Africa for Africans" was the main rallying cry of the day, but the saying was not new in 1920 or unique to the UNIA. In fact, the phrase had been identified with the Pan-African movement since at least 1900. Supporters of this movement believed that black people in the West would only be free if they began an organized move back to Africa and expelled the continent's white colonial rulers.

The roots of the Pan-African movement can be traced back to the American slave trade in the early eighteenth century. As African American historian John Hope Franklin writes, "There was hardly a time when some blacks in the Americas did not hope to return to the land of their forebears."[32]

One of the first people to attempt to realize the Pan-African dream was a wealthy black shipowner, Paul Cuffe of Boston. In 1815 Cuffe accompanied seven African American families to Sierra Leone and arranged for them to acquire fifty acres (20 ha) of land and a year's rations. Cuffe saw the seven families as the beginning of a mass movement of American blacks to Africa. However, Cuffe returned to the United States after several months and little is known about the fate of the people involved in his experiment.

Cuffe died unexpectedly in 1817, but by then the idea of shipping free American blacks to Africa had been adopted by an unlikely source. In 1816 a group of white slave owners and several prominent U.S. citizens, including a Supreme Court justice and several former presidents, helped found the American Colonization Society (ACS) as an alternative to the emancipation of slaves in the United States. Members of this group believed that blacks would never be fully accepted by white American society and that the presence of free blacks in the United States threatened to undermine the institution of slavery. Thus, they reasoned, free blacks were better off in Africa. As one ACS member stated, "We must save the Negroes or the Negroes will ruin us."[33] However, at that time few African Americans were willing to leave the land of their birth for an unknown continent where they did not understand the language or the culture. Throughout the nineteenth century, African Americans resisted the idea of returning to Africa.

The Negro History Movement

In the early years of the twentieth century, the Pan-African movement was able to gain new momentum within the black community as the social status and living conditions of African Americans deteriorated. The impetus of the movement came from a small group of black intellectuals who began producing a large body of literature celebrating Africa's history, culture, and contributions to modern society. This occurred at a time when white society in both the United States and Europe bombarded the black race with notions of inferiority. Africa was referred to as the dark continent, and the popular image of Africans in books, newspapers, and magazines was of savage cannibals running through the jungle, kidnapping white missionaries, and cooking them in giant stewpots. As Milfred C. Fierce writes in *The Pan-African Idea in the United States, 1900–1919*, "Permeating these racist assertions was the notion that Africa's people had contributed nothing to the forward march of civilization and human development. Science confirmed, as far as some Whites were concerned, that Black people and Black culture were only deserving of the most impious, callous, out-of-hand rejection."[34]

To counter these prevailing attitudes, the Negro history movement was promoted by several nationally known organizations, including the American Negro Academy and the Association for the Study of Afro-American Life and History. The aim of the movement was to highlight the positive aspects of Africa and its people. Its supporters spread the message that the ancient civilizations of Africa had developed astronomy, mathematics, and other sciences that formed the foundations of modern society. The organizations also praised the work of black inventors such as George Washington Carver, who developed hundreds of products, including synthetic rubber, adhesives, agricultural mainstays, and dyes.

The most prominent leader of the Negro history movement was Du Bois, who is often referred to as "the Father of Pan-Africanism." Du Bois extolled the glories of Africa's past in editorials in the NAACP newspaper *Crisis* and in his 1914 book *The Negro*. Another well-known black leader, Carter G. Woodson, known as "the Father of Black History," also wrote books on the positive contributions that blacks had made to the development

The Harlem Parade

The UNIA held its annual convention every August. The highlight of the affair was a long parade through Harlem. The 1920 parade was described by Roi Ottley in *New World A-Coming*:

Noisy meetings at Liberty Hall were climaxed by a magnificent parade in which more than fifty thousand Garveyites marched through Harlem. His Excellency, Marcus Garvey, Provisional President of Africa, led the demonstration bedecked in a dazzling uniform of purple, green, and black, with gold braid and a thrilling hat with white plumes, "as long as the leaves of Guinea grass." He rode in a big, high-mounted black Packard automobile and graciously, but with restraint becoming a sovereign, acknowledged the ovations of the crowds that lined the sidewalks. Behind him rode his Grace, Archbishop [Alexander] McGuire, in silk robes of State, blessing the populace. Then the Black Nobility and Knight Commanders of the Distinguished Order of the Nile followed, the hierarchy of the state, properly attired in regalia drawn from a gold palette. Arrayed in gorgeous uniforms of black and green, trimmed with much gold braid came the smartly strutting African Legion.

In his role as provisional president of Africa, Marcus Garvey sports a fancy dress uniform for a parade.

Writer Carter G. Woodson urged African Americans to be proud of their heritage.

of the United States. In addition, he published many magazine articles analyzing the contributions and positive roles of African Americans. In 1926, with a grant of fifty thousand dollars from the philanthropic Carnegie and Rockefeller foundations, Woodson instituted Negro History Week to publicize the accomplishments of black people, a concept established in the present day as Black History Month. Like Du Bois and Garvey, Woodson's message was that black people should be proud of their heritage and that white Americans should be grateful for black contributions to society.

Black Nationalism

This encouraging message struck a nerve and sparked revolutionary fervor in pockets of black American society just as Garvey arrived in the United States. Garvey seized on the concepts of black pride and black identity and infused the Pan-African message with a new element: a call for black separatism, or black nationalism. He proposed that American blacks move to Africa as soon as possible and take control of vast African resources such as oil, iron ore, and rubber that brought great wealth to white industrialists.

However grandiose Garvey's proposals were, he apparently recognized that African Americans might be unwilling to pick up and leave the United States even if they could take over African lands. He remarked jokingly at the 1920 UNIA convention that he did not expect Harlem's blacks to pack their trunks and move to Africa until the organization built large apartment buildings

"American Negroes . . . Were Scandalized"

Although W.E.B. Du Bois was a strong supporter of Pan-Africanism, he strongly disagreed with the methods Garvey used to build black pride. In the following 1923 essay, printed in *Marcus Garvey and the Vision of Africa*, Du Bois voices his disgust with Garvey:

It was upon the tenth of August, in High Harlem. . . . There was a long, low, unfinished church basement, roofed over. [Garvey, a] little, fat black man, ugly, but with intelligent eyes and big head, was seated on a plank platform beside a "throne," dressed in a

military uniform of the gayest mid-Victorian type, heavy with gold lace, epaulets, plume, and sword. Beside him were "potentates," and before him knelt a succession of several colored gentlemen. These in the presence of a thousand or more applauding dark spectators were duly "knighted" and raised to the "peerage" as knight-commanders and dukes of Uganda and the Niger. . . .

What did it all mean? A casual observer might have mistaken it for the dress rehearsal of a new comic opera. . . . But it was not; it was a serious occasion, done on the whole soberly and solemnly. Another might have found it simply silly. . . .

On the other hand, many American negroes . . . were scandalized by something which they could but regard as simply child's play. It seemed to them sinister, this enthroning of a demagogue, a blatant boaster, who with monkey shines was deluding the people and taking their hard-earned dollars.

W.E.B. Du Bois expressed disgust with Marcus Garvey's fascination for uniforms and ceremony.

staffed by bellboys and elevator operators. Relegating the goal of mass migration to the undetermined future, Garvey proposed to first send the best and brightest of Harlem, known as the Talented Tenth. These people were defined as the 10 percent of Harlem residents who were successful doctors, lawyers, architects, and engineers. Once in Africa, they would oversee the construction of railroads, hospitals, and schools in preparation for the masses who would follow. Garvey appealed to the Talented Tenth by stating, "We are going to live for a higher purpose, the purpose of a free and redeemed Africa, because no security, no success can come to the Black man, so long as he is outnumbered."[35]

Garvey was well aware that many obstacles stood in the way of his vision. One obvious problem was that most of Africa was already under the control of Great Britain, France, Belgium, and other colonial powers that were not about to release their grip on the continent. But Garvey believed that under his leadership the black race would rise in revolt, and he seriously proposed that Africa be freed by force, stating, "There is absolutely no reason why [the] 400,000,000 Negroes of the world should not make a desperate effort to re-conquer our Motherland from the white man."[36]

A Project in Liberia

To liberate Africa from white rule, Garvey's master plan first called for establishing a UNIA foothold in the Republic of Liberia. Located on Africa's West Coast, Liberia was Africa's only independent nation, ruled at that time by descendants of African American settlers who moved there in the nineteenth century.

The ambitious Garvey sent a delegation to Liberia, led by UNIA commissioner Elie Garcia. In August 1920 Garcia filed a confidential report of his trip that assessed conditions in the African nation. Liberia, he reported, was rich in natural resources but desperately poor by every other measure; in fact, it was one of the poorest countries on Earth, and its people were facing starvation. For this he blamed the so called Americo-Liberians, the descendants of the original African American settlers. According to Garcia, the Americo-Liberians all worked in vast government bureaucracies, earning salaries while taking bribes, skimming

Pan-Africanism Defined

———————■———————

Although the idea of Pan-Africanism has taken many forms, there are three overriding beliefs that define the movement. In *The Pan-African Movement: A History of Pan-Africanism in America, Europe, and Africa*, Imanuel Geiss provides a definition. Pan-Africanism consists of:

1. Intellectual and political movements among Africans and Afro-Americans who regard . . . Africans and people of African descent as homogeneous. This outlook leads to a feeling of racial solidarity and a new self-awareness and causes Afro-Americans to look upon Africa as their real "homeland," without necessarily thinking of a physical return to Africa.

2. All ideas which have stressed . . . the cultural unity and political independence of Africa, including the desire to modernize Africa on a basis of equality of rights. The key concepts here have been respectively the "redemption of Africa" and "Africa for the Africans."

3. Ideas or political movements which have advocated . . . the political unity of Africa or at least close political collaboration in one form or another.

taxes, and using native Liberians as slaves. As Garcia wrote, "They buy men and women to serve them and the least little insignificant Americo-Liberian has half a dozen boys at his service. . . . He will not even carry his own umbrella down in the street."[37] Meanwhile, the nation's rulers practiced polygamy and bought and sold young girls for use as sex slaves.

In addition to widespread corruption and social ills, Liberia had virtually no infrastructure. Garcia argued that immigration to Liberia could only commence after about four hundred thousand dollars was invested in roads, railroads, shipping lines, and other ventures. This would not only improve the prospects of the UNIA, but it would also "win the inalienable devotion of the

Liberian people and of the people of the West Coast [of Africa] in general."[38] However, the commissioner warned that the Liberian rulers would be violently "opposed to any element which may be instrumental in bringing to [an] end their political tyranny, their habits of graft, and their polygamic freedom."[39]

Garcia recommended that the UNIA proceed cautiously with plans to send members to Liberia who would conceal their intentions from the nation's leaders. Garvey set out to raise $2 million for the UNIA Liberia project.

In March 1921 the first delegation of UNIA officials and workers arrived in Liberia to select sites and draw up plans for farms, buildings, a drug store, and other basic elements of a core community. Liberian cabinet ministers, at first indifferent, offered to sell a few hundred acres to the delegation. However, British and French officials expressed alarm, fearing that American blacks were going to attempt to take over Africa using Liberia as their base. This prompted Liberian president C.D.B. King to write an editorial in *Crisis* stating that Liberia would not allow itself to become the center of aggression against other African nations.

From Harlem, Garvey continued to raise money for the Liberian project. However, in March 1922 Garcia's secret report—with its frank assessments of Liberian society—was published in the New York newspaper the *African World*. It is unclear who leaked the confidential document; regardless, its publication did little to improve relations between Liberia and the UNIA. By 1924 relations had deteriorated to such a point that the Liberian consul in New York announced that Garveyites would not be permitted to disembark in Liberia. Several who tried were immediately arrested and deported. By the end of 1924, Garvey's Liberia project was dead.

"Negro Representatives"

The scheme to settle in Liberia was only one of many UNIA projects meant to build black nationhood under UNIA leadership, in line with a resolution passed during the first UNIA convention in 1920. This resolution, called the Declaration of Rights of the Negro Peoples of the World, stated that the "Negro people of the world . . . protest against the wrongs and injustices they are suffering at the hands of their white brethren."[40] Claiming to be the duly elected representatives of the world's entire black population, the UNIA affirmed that it would appoint delegates to act as ambassadors and called the world's nations to "accept and acknowledge Negro representatives who shall be sent to said governments to represent the general welfare of the Negro peoples throughout the world."[41]

This bold, if not delusional, attempt to establish a government in exile complete with ambassadors was put to the test in 1922 when European leaders met in Switzerland to decide the fate of German colonies in Africa that were forfeited after Germany's defeat in World War I. The UNIA sent a distinguished delegation to the conference that included an Oxford graduate from Sierra Leone, college professors from Trinidad and Jamaica, and several eminent African American scholars. When the delegation arrived in Geneva, it presented a petition requesting German colonies be signed over to black people since black soldiers had helped defeat Germany in the war. The UNIA delegates were seated among delegates of other nations, but their efforts came to nothing after many months of effort.

In 1924 Garvey continued his efforts to legitimize the concept of black nationhood by sending Richard Hilton

Liberian president C.D.B. King did not want his country used as a base for aggression against neighboring nations.

Marcus Garvey relied on the power of the written word to sway his followers.

Tobitt, a former African Methodist Episcopal minister in Bermuda, to London to act as a UNIA ambassador to Great Britain. Garvey bestowed on Tobitt the title of knight-commander of the Sublime Order of the Nile and addressed him formally as Sir Richard Hilton Tobitt. With his usual flair for the extravagant, Garvey sent the British government a letter explaining that Tobitt was the "High Commissioner and Minister Plenipotentiary to His Britannic Majesty's Government." He was in England to "interest himself in all matters affecting the interest of the Negro race within Great Britain."[42] Despite Tobitt's grand title and lofty purpose, his requests to meet with the British prime minister and the secretary of state were rejected. According to an unnamed British official, the government would not meet with the UNIA official because the organization "has a record of fraud, sedition, and incitement to violence."[43]

Great Britain was not alone in refusing to recognize official UNIA representatives. Other so-called ambassadors were met with outright hostility even in Trinidad, where the organization had a large following. For the most part, the UNIA presumption of nationhood was viewed with amusement or was completely confused with little-known foreign governments. For example, when President Warren G. Harding died in office in 1923, the UNIA sent a funeral delegation in a large Packard convertible to Washington, D.C. The group was mistaken for representatives from a sovereign African nation and was allowed to ride in the president's funeral procession. After the ceremony was over, the delegation, complete with UNIA members riding on the Packard's running boards, drove through the streets of Washington. Police stopped traffic to give their car right-of-way and saluted the delegation as it passed. Never before had the African Americans in the car been treated with such respect by southern policemen.

"Sowing Seeds of Discontent"

Garvey may have failed to convince high-level government officials that he was the provisional president of Africa, but he had no such trouble among the people he claimed to represent. As a prolific writer, he was able to utilize the *Negro World* to promote black nationalism, unity, and pride. When critics made negative accusations that the paper was promoting propaganda, Garvey embraced the word, saying "We are not afraid of the word *propaganda* . . . for we use the term in the sense of disseminating our ideas among Negroes all the world over."[44]

Each weekly issue of the *Negro World* featured a full front-page editorial by Garvey. This was followed by columns from some of the most highly regarded black writers of the Harlem Renaissance, including Zora Neale Hurston, W.A. Domingo, T. Thomas Fortune, and Arthur Schomburg.

Unlike other African American newspaper publishers at the time, Garvey's strong belief in black pride and black beauty and

AT LAST THE DAY HAS COME

Negro Money, Negro Brains, and Negro Energy Must Rule The World

Mr. Black Man, what are you doing to insure a bright future for the race? Are you investing your money wisely as to turn over profits for you and your children and posterity?

Now is the chance for you to do something real. Invest some of the money you have in the Bank, at home, or in your pocket in

The Negro Factories Corporation

This Corporation is to build factories all over the United States, Canada, West Indies, South and Central America, and Africa.

This Corporation is organized under the State Laws of Delaware, and capitalized at $1,000,000. You may buy as many shares as you desire at $5.00 each.

The Negro Factories Corporation will offer employment to thousands of Negroes. The Factories will manufacture goods of all kinds, to be sold in American Markets, and shipped by the Black Star Line Steamship to foreign countries

Buy your shares to-day, make money and put up a factory in your neighborhood to be owned and controlled by the Race.

Send in or call for your shares at

THE NEGRO FACTORIES CORPORATION
56 W. 135th Street, New York, U. S. A.

A notice in the *Negro World* urges investors to buy stock in Garvey's company.

his rejection of white standards of beauty prevented him from advertising skin bleaches and hair straighteners. While advertisements from manufacturers of these kinds of products provided the majority of revenue to papers such as the *Chicago Defender* and the *Baltimore Afro-American*, Garvey was forced to absorb the share of the newspaper's production costs that would have been paid for by this advertising.

The *Negro World* presented Garvey's Pan-African perspective to black readers across the globe. It was printed in French in Trinidad, in Spanish in Cuba, and in English in Jamaica, the United States, and even Australia. Issues of the paper also appeared in Kenya, Dahomey (modern-day Benin), Nigeria, Gambia, and other African nations.

Officially, however, the newspaper was disapproved of; the paper was banned in many countries, and readers caught with copies were jailed. A report from the British Colonial Office in 1924 explains why the British suppressed the *Negro World*:

> The [paper] has occupied itself for some years in propaganda among the negros in the United States, the West Indies and . . . West Africa with the object of [advocating] among them a sense of "nationality" and of sowing seeds of discontent and revolt against their existing conditions of life. The [UNIA] movement deliberately attempts to foment racial antagonism and has assumed a seditious and revolutionary aspect, which finds expression in . . . the "Negro World."[45]

In Costa Rica, officials outlawed the paper, claiming it was promoting race riots, revolution, and Bolshevism. In Trinidad, authorities confiscated stacks of the *Negro World* from local post offices and burned them. People in possession of the paper in Nigeria, Gambia, or Panama could be jailed; a person caught with the *Negro World* in Dahomey could be sentenced to life in prison. Despite these harsh penalties, the paper was distributed clandestinely in many nations by students, sailors, and laborers. By 1923 weekly circulation of the *Negro World* had grown to two hundred thousand, and the paper was the most influential and widely read black weekly in the world.

"A Wonderful Civilization"

While government officials feared Garvey's brand of Pan-Africanism, his words gave hope to hundreds of thousands of poor black laborers throughout the world. Perhaps for the first time in their lives, they were able to read that black history did not begin with slavery but with a glorious past in Africa, a past that gave birth to Western civilization. As Garvey wrote:

> When the great white race of today had no civilization of its own, when white men lived in caves and were counted as savages, this race of ours boasted of a wonderful civilization on the Banks of the Nile. . . . This race of ours gave civilization, gave art, gave science, gave literature to the world. . . . The Negro once occupied a high position in the world, scientifically, artistically and commercially, but in the balancing of the great scale of evolution, we lost our place.[46]

Garvey's greatest talent was as a preacher and a propagandist, and his great plan was in many ways unrealistic. But for a few short years in the 1920s, the dream of an independent black nation in Africa seemed within grasp as the Pan-African message took hold on both sides of the Atlantic Ocean.

Chapter Four

The UNIA Mission: Black Enterprise and African Nationhood

Marcus Garvey's Pan-African message of racial pride, black nationalism, and black nationhood was interpreted by government authorities as a call to anarchy, not unity. There was widespread, general suspicion of all political dissent at this time, not just racial dissent. In 1917 the czarist government in Russia had been overthrown by Bolshevik revolutionaries who established the world's first Communist state. Many Americans feared a similar revolution might be brewing in the United States. Justice Department officials used the threat of communism as a reason to spy on political dissidents of all kinds, including Marcus Garvey and members of the UNIA. J. Edgar Hoover, special assistant to Attorney General Mitchell Palmer and later director of the FBI, justified the focus on Garvey by saying that in the *Negro World*, "Soviet Russian Rule is upheld, and there is an open advocation of Bolshevism."[47]

Yet communism held little attraction for Garvey, who believed in private ownership of land and businesses. Besides, as Theodore Kornweibel Jr. writes in *Seeing Red: Federal Campaigns Against Black Militancy, 1919–1925*, "While Garvey applauded global turmoil [the Russian Revolution] as presaging the day when Africa would be liberated, communism was no more trustworthy than any other white-led movement or philosophy. A white communist was a white man first, and as such deserved no confidence."[48] What Garvey was actually promoting among black people was a version of the so-called American dream, in which people achieved prosperity, property ownership, and personal freedom through hard work and smart, open-market business practices. Garvey put his faith in capitalism, an economic system directly opposed to communism, to accomplish these goals.

Garvey had incorporated the UNIA and the African Communities League in 1918 with an eye toward profit. He aimed to get rich, and to help other black people get rich, through business management and investment. Many UNIA supporters were middle-class blacks who agreed with this strategy and used group meetings to discuss economic opportunities and strengthen business and political connections. There was a more radical wing of the UNIA that advocated Socialist or Communist policies, but Garvey did not endorse their views, expressing his pro-business beliefs in a 1919 *Negro World* editorial: "If we are . . . to become a great national force, we must start business enterprises of our own; we must build ships and start trading with ourselves between America, the West Indies, and Africa."[49]

The Black Star Line

In February 1919 the UNIA began its first moneymaking venture, a Harlem restaurant. This small business was hardly profitable enough to enable the UNIA to "build ships and start trading." To that end, Garvey created the Black Star Line (BSL) Steamship Corporation in May 1919. He viewed the shipping line as a symbol of economic and political power and took the U.S. Shipping Board as his management model. This agency managed a fleet of thirteen hundred commercial vessels that were profiting handsomely from new shipping opportunities in expanding foreign markets. Trade between the United States and Africa had jumped nearly sevenfold between 1914 and 1919, and raw materials from Africa were unloaded at docks in New York City every day. However, like most other white-owned enterprises, the shipping business openly discriminated against African Americans in its own workforce and customer base.

Black seamen were forced to live in substandard conditions compared with white sailors. They were the last to be hired during times of economic growth and the first to be fired when business slowed. Black passengers, even those possessing first-class tickets, traveled in segregated quarters, were denied entrance into ship saloons, and could not even eat in dining rooms until white passengers were finished. In the West Indies and Africa, white corporations denied black merchants and agricultural producers the profitable shipping rights to markets in the United States and Europe.

Garvey's Black Star Line was founded to right these wrongs while building a strong economic foundation for black independence. The ships would also be used, Garvey announced, to transport thousands of African Americans to Africa along with food, machinery, clothing, and other necessities. However, building a shipping line was a complicated and expensive venture. Even a moderately sized vessel easily cost from $150,000 to $500,000 at a time when the average worker made about $8 a day. When no bank would lend money to Garvey for this venture, he began to sell BSL stock to the public.

Garvey's stock offering occurred at the beginning of the stock market boom that took place during the Roaring Twenties. In the following years millions of average Americans invested in stocks for the first time, and a few got rich overnight. The fever for rampant speculation affected black investors as well as white ones. In 1921 editors of the *New York Age* warned:

> The craze for buying stocks . . . has become almost epidemic in Harlem. Individuals who have laid aside a comfortable nest egg in the savings bank . . . have exchanged the certainty of four percent [return on their investment] for the hopeful anticipation of at least ten or perhaps twenty percent dividends from some unproved oil well or doubtful industrial enterprise.[50]

"We Will Have Something to Offer"

Marcus Garvey often preached that black people must establish and work for black-owned businesses. The following speech before six thousand UNIA members, gathered at a rally for the Black Star Line Steamship Corporation in May 1920, is printed in volume two of *The Marcus Garvey and Universal Negro Improvement Association Papers*:

> We are now in a new age. We are now in a new era. . . . And if we in America and in Africa can build up republics, can build up [mills], can build up factories, can build up steamboat lines, we will give the lie to those Crackers of the south who said that the Negro can follow white leaders but not leaders of his own: We want to demonstrate in the twentieth century that under the guidance [and] leadership of black men, following the plans of black men, the plans of Negro brains, working with Negro hands, we can do all in the commercial world that other men and races can do.
>
> When you can build yourselves up commercially in New York you won't have to worry about having a Negro representative in Congress. When you make yourselves factors in the commercial life of Philadelphia and in Chicago, you won't have to worry about having a Negro representative in Congress. . . . And it is because, through Marcus Garvey, two great movements have been launched which shows that the Negro is entering an era of achievement, that we will write a new page upon the world's history. And instead of begging other nations and races for a chance, we will have them coming to us, because we will have something to offer.

Garvey's timing could not have been better. When he offered ownership in the Black Star Line for only five dollars a share, thousands of black investors seized the opportunity to buy BSL stock in the belief that they were not only going to get rich but that their investment was contributing to the betterment of the

Garvey sought investors for his Black Star Line, as seen in this newspaper announcement.

race and advancing the Pan-African cause. Writing in 1938, Jamaican author Lens Nembhard provides a common view of the BSL proposal held by Garvey's supporters:

Soon the Negroes would have their own ships. Luxurious liners which would be officered by men of their own race. On pleasure cruises or on visits to their native land, there would be no cringing in the lounge to give the white man way. Above all, when the time came, as it would surely come, from the decks of their own vessels, they would wave farewell, throwing a parting kiss, to foreign fields and friends and steam out to a glorious life in Africa.[51]

Garvey set out to establish the Black Star Line in record time, planning to raise $2 million by September 1919 and launch the first BSL ships on October 31. Lucky investors, he told an audience in Detroit, would realize great profits:

The Black Star Line Corporation presents to every Black Man, Woman, and Child the opportunity to climb the great ladder of industrial and commercial progress. If you have ten dollars, one hundred dollars, or one or five thousand dollars to invest for profit, then take out shares in the Black Star Line, Inc. This corporation is chartered to trade on every sea and all waters. The Black Star Line will turn over large profits and dividends to stockholders, and operate to their interest even whilst they will be asleep.[52]

UNIA members crisscrossed the country selling shares in the Black Star Line. Promising riches and freedom, they managed to raise enough money to purchase the first BSL ship by September 17. In the meantime, the Black Star Line was incorporated in Delaware and an office was set up on 135th Street in Harlem.

A Bad Buy

While generating great optimism among its supporters, the success of the Black Star Line was hardly assured. The vessel seemed like a good value to the BSL board of directors, which approved its purchase for $165,000. Problems soon became apparent, however. The thirty-two-year-old vessel, named *Yarmouth*, had been used as a coal and cattle boat in World War I. It was filthy and unsuitable for passenger service, a drawback apparently overlooked by the purchasers. According to Elton C. Fax in *Garvey: The Story of a Pioneer Black Nationalist*, "Garvey and his board of directors . . . knew as much about ships as they did about interplanetary space travel."[53] Their lack of business acumen made them an easy target for the *Yarmouth's* original owner, a white cotton broker named W.L. Harriss, who paid the ship's black captain, Joshua Cockburn, $1,600 to swear the vessel was a good buy. However, according to the assessment of another black officer, the *Yarmouth* was not seaworthy and not worth more than $25,000 for scrap.

The Black Star Line faced other problems with its flagship. Harriss had sold the *Yarmouth* for payment terms of $16,500 down and $83,500 due when the UNIA took possession of the ship. The remaining $65,000 was due in a series of ten payments at 6 percent interest. Until the payments were made, Harriss retained ownership of the *Yarmouth*.

Ignoring the unfavorable terms and the condition of the ship, Garvey renamed the *Yarmouth* the SS *Frederick Douglass* after the famous nineteenth-century abolitionist. He announced that the vessel would soon set sail for the West Indies. However, Harriss would not let the ship sail without insurance, and Garvey could not find anyone to insure it.

The public was unaware of the difficulties facing the Black Star Line. When Garvey announced that the *Frederick Douglass* would be launched from Harlem's 135th Street dock on October 31, several thousand enthusiastic UNIA members and supporters were in attendance. Admittedly, the uninsured ship floated only as far as 23rd Street, but the maiden voyage was declared a success nevertheless.

Adulation, Sabotage, and Mismanagement

In the ensuing months the Black Star Line limped along, supported by public adulation and Garvey's promotional skills and crippled by internal sabotage and financial mismanagement. Eventually the ship was insured, and the *Frederick Douglass* left New York on November 24, destined for Cuba with a cargo of cement. It also carried several passengers who were among the company's largest stockholders. When the ship reached the Cuban city of Sagua la Grande, it was greeted by hundreds of cheering supporters. Black Star salesmen fanned out through the crowd and managed to sell thousands of dollars' worth of BSL stock.

In January 1920 the ship was commissioned to transport a $5-million supply of whiskey to Cuba. For this voyage Cockburn charged only $11,000, a sum described by another Black Star captain, Hugh Mulzac, as "insufficient to even get [the ship] to her destination let alone return dividends for the poor stockholders."[54] A few miles out of port, the ship was deliberately sabotaged by an engineer, most likely at Cockburn's order. Claiming the ship was foundering, the captain ordered five hundred cases of whiskey thrown overboard. These were fished out of the water and carried away by men on small boats who were undoubtedly part of a plan to steal the valuable cargo.

Mechanical breakdowns, conflicts with officials, and other problems dogged the *Frederick Douglass* on later voyages. Nonetheless, wherever the ship traveled, it was enthusiastically greeted by black supporters, often bearing baskets of food and flowers for the crew. Although the cargoes were losing money, the crowds enthusiastically snapped up shares of BSL

Why the Black Star Line Failed

The Black Star Line Steamship Corporation was plagued by incompetence at all levels that spelled financial disaster for its investors. In *A Star to Steer By*, Hugh Mulzac, a captain on the Black Star Line, describes the corporation's failures and the resulting fallout:

> Not one of the company's officers had the most rudimentary understanding of the shipping business. . . . The executive positions in the company were staffed by opportunists and relatives from all walks of life except the shipping industry. Ocean commerce, especially in the '20's, was one of the most highly [efficient] industries in the world . . . and many large and efficiently-run companies engaged in cargo trade. . . . To compete with such companies effectively meant having good ships, sound capital backing, an extensive network of good agents, and above all efficient management. . . .
>
> The [Black Star Line flagship] *Yarmouth* lost hundreds of thousands of dollars putting into ports where no cargo awaited, and in being chartered below her worth.
>
> Thus the great and bold dream of colored resurgence ended in catastrophe. For their hard-won dollars scores of thousands of humble black men and women received in dividends only a transitory inflation of their racial pride. . . .
>
> What had begun as a great adventure for me and hundreds of thousands of others ended in tragedy and disillusionment. It was difficult to compute the suffering that resulted from this idealism. Thousands had mortgaged their homes to buy Black Star stock, others had sold their furniture and possessions to buy passage to Africa on ships that would never leave port. . . . Dollars evaporated with the dreams, personal ambitions with the hopes and aspirations of a whole people.

Black Star's *Yarmouth* (pictured) was purchased with the intent of transporting American blacks to Africa in style.

stock. A typical scene in Bocas del Toro, Panama, was described by Mulzac:

[Thousands] of peasants came down from the hills on horses, donkeys, and in makeshift carts, and by a special train provided by the United Fruit Company, which, since it was going to lose its employees for the day anyway, declared a legal holiday. The crowd on the dock was so thick that when we threw our heavy lines ashore the peasants seized the hangers as they came out of the water and literally breasted us alongside the dock. In the tumult that followed dancing broke out on the deck, great piles of fruit and flowers mounted on the hatch covers, and U.N.I.A. agents signed up hundreds of new members.[55]

But the fervor of peasant crowds could not keep the troubled *Frederick Douglass* afloat. By the end of 1920, the ship was seized by U.S. marshals over unpaid repair bills of $75,000. It was sold by federal agents just two years after its first UNIA voyage for a paltry $1625.

The End of the Black Star Line

The Black Star Line purchased two other ships that were similarly doomed. The thirty-five-thousand-dollar *Shadyside*, built in 1872, came into the company's possession in April 1920. This vessel was ostensibly purchased to take black passengers on day trips on New York's Hudson River. Its real purpose was to be a showpiece that would help spur BSL stock sales. However, after several excursions the *Shadyside* was moored in Fort Lee, New Jersey, for the winter. Damaged during an ice storm, the aged ship sank when a seam in its hull split open.

Around the same time that the *Shadyside* was purchased, the Black Star Line bought the SS *Kanawha*. Because of the expenses incurred by the *Frederick Douglass*, the newest ship in the Black Star Line was much smaller, actually classified as a yacht. This boat also proved to be another mechanical disaster. Before it was purchased, Boston UNIA member Captain Adrian Richardson inspected the boat and warned that its steam boilers were in terrible shape and that it would cost more to operate and repair than it could be expected to earn. Garvey brushed aside this assessment, went ahead with the purchase, and hired Richardson to captain the ship.

The words of Richardson came back to haunt Garvey on the *Kanawha's* maiden cruise on the Hudson when the ship's boiler blew up and killed a crew member. Throughout 1920 and 1921 the *Kanawha* was plagued by other mechanical failures during a series of ill-fated voyages to Cuba, South America, and elsewhere. Most problems went unrepaired by the inexperienced crew hired by the Black Star Line, which by now could not afford skilled sailors, mechanics, and engineers. The poorly paid and mostly unqualified crew members were often found drinking, gambling, and even fighting on deck in full view of horrified passengers. Finally, in the summer of 1921, the *Kanawha* broke down in Cuba and was abandoned. Thieves stripped the ship of valuable parts, and the *Kanawha* half sank during a storm. In April 1922 an article in the *Negro World* announced the end of the star-crossed Black Star Line.

The Negro Factories Corporation

While Garvey's attempts to keep his hapless shipping company afloat failed, between 1919 and 1922 the UNIA was also running several other businesses that, perhaps because of their grassroots origins and wider community involvement, proved much more successful than the Black Star Line.

In 1919 the UNIA founded the Negro Factories Corporation (NFC). Under the auspices of this corporation, the UNIA established the Universal Laundries, the Universal Millinery Store, Universal Restaurants, Universal Grocery Stores, a hotel, a tailoring business, a printer, and even a doll factory. As he had done

The NFC promoted African American-owned businesses in Harlem and allowed them to successfully compete with white-owned businesses.

with the Black Star Line, Garvey used the *Negro World* to publicize the NFC and to raise funds through a stock offering. Writing that the NFC was going to "build and operate factories in the big industrial centers of the United States, Central America, the West Indies, and Africa to manufacture every marketable commodity,"[56] Garvey offered two hundred thousand shares of common stock to supporters at five dollars per share.

After raising about two hundred thousand dollars the Negro Factories Corporation bought three buildings and two trucks and began operations. Within a year the NFC employed three hundred people and was considering the purchase of its own bank. By 1924 the NFC employed more than one thousand people in the United States and hundreds more throughout the world.

Even as the Black Star Line became a symbol of ineptitude, fraud, and mismanagement, by 1922 the NFC had become a symbol of African American business acumen in Harlem. Using a single, experienced manager to buy food for both the NFC restaurants and grocery stores, Universal Grocery Stores and Universal Restaurants were able to successfully compete with white-owned businesses.

Creative marketing helped the grocery stores appeal to both black and white customers. At a time when most people shopped at a butcher shop for meat, a fish store for seafood, and a produce stand for vegetables, the Universal Grocery Store No. 3 on Lenox in Harlem offered meat, fish, and vegetables under one roof. The store also expanded its merchandise to attract customers with

Bypassing White Middlemen

Black farmers who sold their products to the Negro Factories Corporation risked their livelihoods—and sometimes their lives—when they stopped dealing with the white shippers and distributors who previously had held a monopoly on trade. In *Time Longer than Rope: A Century of African American Activism,* Winston James describes the situation:

> Black Southern farmers sold their sweet yams and other farm produce directly to the UNIA [Negro Factories Corporation], bypassing white middlemen and their greed; courageous defiance of Southern conventions, which . . . could have cost these Southern members "economic reprisals at best and physical horror at worst" [according to UNIA executive J. Raymond Jones]. With similar audacity, some in Florida sold oranges and grapefruits to the organization. And from the Caribbean still others sold limes to the Negro Factories Corporation. On one occasion, two members in Georgia contacted UNIA headquarters and sought the Corporation's help in selling two rail tanks of molasses. Jones, who was by this time an avid reader of the *Journal of Commerce*, knew what to do and successfully disposed of the cargo for a good price to the American Molasses Company on Wall Street. Expenses were deducted and the money was sent to his happy UNIA brethren in Georgia. From Africa, farmers in Ghana sent word that they would like to sell their cocoa to the UNIA, thus bypassing the commodities sharks in London.

American South, Caribbean, and African backgrounds, stocking West Indian yams, plantains, southern sweet potatoes, and taro root. In addition, all Universal Grocery Stores employed black butchers, cashiers, stock boys, managers, and maintenance workers.

Universal Restaurant No. 1 was located in the heart of the UNIA community, at Liberty Hall. The restaurant, with a seating capacity of one hundred, was managed by Mary Lawrence, a food chemist who had previously been employed as a dietitian in a hospital. A second Universal Restaurant on 135th Street was less successful, facing stiff competition from more than half a dozen other eating establishments in the immediate area.

The Negro Factories Corporation made inroads in several other retail and manufacturing areas. The Bee Hive Printing Plant, for example, quickly became the leading press in Harlem. Within a year of its establishment, Bee Hive was printing the majority of the brochures, magazines, letterheads, and other materials for Harlem's black business community. The company also published more than one hundred thousand copies of the *Negro World* every week.

On West 142nd Street, a building called the Universal Mart of Industry housed the Universal Steam and Electric Laundry, described by Garvey as "one of the best equipped and up-to-date laundries operated by any race."[57] Ads for the laundry in the *Negro World* boasted that work was performed by "Negro Experts in a Modern Sanitary Steam Laundry" and promised to "Return Everything Except the Dirt."[58]

The Universal Mart of Industry was also the site of the Men's Manufacturing Department and the Women's Manufacturing Department and Bazaar. Both enterprises made UNIA medals, insignias, and uniforms. The men's department also produced Panama hats, shirts, ties, and other clothing items. These goods could be purchased by mail order, and plans were in the works to create a mail-order catalog business for other NFC products.

The offices of the corporation provided employment opportunities that were denied to black workers elsewhere in American society, where African Americans were largely limited to unskilled labor jobs. Hundreds of young black men and women worked at the Negro Factories Corporation as office managers, clerks, accountants, stenographers, and secretaries.

Beyond those seeking employment opportunities, the NFC attracted black businesspeople, many of whom were struggling financially, applying for loans. Garvey's well-intentioned efforts to help black people achieve economic independence, however, often led him to invest in faltering businesses without investigating their viability. The NFC also bought real estate such as offices and empty factories to rent to black entrepreneurs, and the reach of the organization eventually extended well beyond Harlem. By 1924 the UNIA owned property in Philadelphia, Pittsburgh, Chicago, Detroit, and Colón, Panama. In Kingston, Jamaica, the NFC ran a laundry and a bank financed by shares sold to UNIA members.

While profits helped inspire workers of the NFC, most were motivated by the belief that black business ventures could finance one great independence movement. Garvey noted this when he wrote in 1920, "All these [financial achievements] to the ordinary optimist would seem a miracle, but all these things have been accomplished through the determination of the men and women who banded themselves together as members of the movement. Wherever there is a will there is a way, and the will of the new Negro is to do or die."[59] This belief was the driving force behind the UNIA and Pan-Africanism. According to Garvey, faced with the combined economic power of black business enterprises, white society could no longer ignore the "men and women who are able to create, to originate and improve, and thus make an independent racial contribution to the world and civilization."[60]

Chapter Five

Women Take the Leading Roles

Under Marcus Garvey's leadership, the Universal Negro Improvement Association acquired a historical image as male dominated, but in fact women made up half the membership in the UNIA. In some chapters women were a majority of members. According to Barbara Bair on the Public Broadcasting Service's Web site:

> Women proved to be the backbone of the Garvey movement . . . [active] on many levels. . . . They served as delegates to international conventions, representing their local divisions, and argued their viewpoints from the floor. . . . Women served as UNIA regional, national, and international organizers and as local officers. They sold stock for the Black Star Line and helped arrange and run UNIA programs and meetings. Every local branch had a "lady president." And, individual women were stars in the national and international leadership of the UNIA.[61]

Two capable women in particular—both named Amy—had a profound influence not only on the UNIA but on the Pan-

African movement throughout the twentieth century. The first was Amy Ashwood of Kingston, Jamaica, who met Garvey in July 1914 at the weekly meeting of the East Queen Street Baptist Literary and Debating Society. Although Ashwood was only seventeen years old, she was already passionately committed to the cause of black liberation. Garvey asked Ashwood to become the secretary of the organization he was forming, and the young woman accepted his offer. The next week, Ashwood became the first member of the UNIA and member of the board of management. She later wrote that she and Garvey "planned a great Black Confraternity, under our own vine and fig tree in our own Africa."[62] As to her relationship with Garvey, Ashwood described it as a "bond of comradeship based upon a common idea and belief, directed to a common goal."[63]

Ashwood's middle-class parents were scandalized by their teenage daughter's association with the twenty-seven-year-old Garvey. He was a poor man and, worse, was seen as a troublemaker. Over the objections of the Ashwoods, Garvey courted Amy by composing love poems for her. However, after the two became engaged in 1916, Amy was sent away to Panama by her parents. At this point the Jamaican UNIA only had about one hundred members, and Garvey, discouraged by his failing fortunes in Kingston, soon moved to Harlem.

In September 1918 Ashwood and Garvey were reunited when the young woman followed her fiancé to New York. In Harlem, Ashwood resumed her central role in the UNIA, which was growing rapidly. In addition to working as Garvey's chief aide, Ashwood served as secretary-general of the UNIA, fund-raiser, associate editor of the *Negro World*, and officer of both the Black Star Line Steamship Corporation and the Negro Factories Corporation. Ashwood also worked to include women at all levels of the UNIA, as biographer Ula Yvette Taylor writes:

> The UNIA's constitution was very different from that of most black organizations in that women were well integrated into the movement's structure. Amy Ashwood must be credited with helping to develop a system in which women could enjoy equal participation. Each local division elected a male and female president and vice president.[64]

Taking the Reins of Leadership

As an organization cofounded by Amy Ashwood Garvey, the UNIA gave female members unprecedented powers at a time when gender roles were strictly enforced in society at large. On the Public Broadcasting Service's Web site, civil rights activist and author Barbara Bair describes the treatment of women within the UNIA:

> In the abstract, [Marcus Garvey] lauded the women in the movement. He recognized their importance . . . in sharp and welcome contrast to the negative white stereotypes that demeaned and degraded black femininity. The UNIA as a whole heralded the importance of black motherhood and the nurturing of black children, in part as a remedy and counter balance to the violence, repression, poverty and racism faced in daily lives. They also took very seriously the political contribution of women raising and educating black children to pride and knowledge of the history of their race.
>
> Many women embraced these roles and images, including the idea of black women as beautiful and the centrality and worth of motherhood. . . . But they also wanted more. Garvey, for all his recognition of women and his attitudes of chivalry, relegated them to secondary status. Few women made it into the upper echelons of leadership, and those that did sometimes had a very hard row to hoe. . . . Over time, many Garveyite women became frustrated with the sexism in the movement, and called on each other to, if necessary, sweep ineffectual men aside and take the reins of leadership into their own hands.

The UNIA encouraged participation by its women members, some of whom appear in this photograph.

"Unable to Continue the Old Partnership"

Amy Ashwood and Marcus Garvey were finally married in an elaborate wedding ceremony attended by several thousand guests at Liberty Hall on Christmas Day 1919. Ashwood's maid of honor was her roommate and friend from Jamaica, Amy Jacques, who had also recently immigrated to New York.

Since the Garveys were profoundly dedicated to the fortunes of the UNIA, their honeymoon was more of a working vacation than a romantic getaway. The two were accompanied by several associates and friends, including Jacques, and the group traveled to Canada where they conducted UNIA business in Toronto and Montreal. After the honeymoon, Garvey moved into his wife's apartment, which Jacques continued to share.

It appears that Garvey's rapidly rising fame and the unprecedented growth of the UNIA had a negative effect on the marriage. According to Ashwood Garvey, "In the full glare of the limelight the Marcus Garvey I knew receded into the shadows. The public figure Garvey took his place, and we found we were unable to continue the old partnership."[65]

On March 6, 1920, after only a few months of marriage, Marcus Garvey filed for an annulment. By all accounts the breakup was bitter. Garvey accused his wife of misappropriating funds from the Black Star Line to buy a house in Harlem and also claimed that she had been unfaithful to him. In return, Ashwood Garvey accused her husband of conducting an affair with Amy Jacques, which Garvey vigorously denied.

The end of the Garveys' marriage delighted the many critics of the UNIA and generated headlines in many cities. To quiet the publicity, the Garveys delayed their official divorce until 1922. After their separation, Ashwood Garvey distanced herself from her former husband's activities but continued to work for Pan-African and feminist causes for the rest of her life. In the late 1920s she worked with West Africans to oppose colonialism. In the 1930s she owned a restaurant in London that was a central meeting place for Pan-Africanists.

"Without Restrictions from Men"

In the months following the Garveys' separation, Amy Jacques was hired to work as the UNIA leader's private secretary. According to

Amy Ashwood Garvey worked for Pan-African and feminist causes throughout her life.

government agents who were keeping Garvey under surveillance, the couple were living together as "man and wife."[66] In July 1922, two weeks after his divorce from Ashwood Garvey was finalized, Garvey married Jacques during a small, private ceremony.

At the time, the UNIA claimed more than 6 million members with nine hundred branches throughout the world. In Harlem alone the organization claimed 35,000 members. Though these figures have been questioned, it is generally accepted that no other black nationalist organization in history had ever been as popular. Marcus Garvey was the undisputed, charismatic leader of the UNIA. The new Mrs. Garvey remained out of the limelight unlike Ashwood Garvey, who had often appeared on the podium with her husband.

While Jacques Garvey did not take an immediate public position in the UNIA, other women had higher profiles. On August 21, 1922, for example, during the UNIA annual convention, female members celebrated "Women's Day at Liberty Hall." During a forum called the New Social Policy for the Negro, UNIA women formulated policies to ensure that children were raised to value the highest moral standards. Manners, morality, and honesty were seen as crucial necessities for those founding a new black nation in Africa.

Other than these discussions, Women's Day was given over to exhibitions featuring what were considered traditional female concerns such as arts and crafts and fashion revues. However, ten days later, on the last day of the convention, Victoria W. Turner

Saving Garvey's Life

◼

Marcus Garvey's first wife, Amy Ashwood Garvey, played an integral role in the UNIA in its early years. She was celebrated for her skills as a fund-raiser, as the editor of the *Negro World*, and as an officer of several UNIA corporations. Several months before she married Garvey in December 1919, she also helped foil a purported assassination attempt on her future husband's life. The story is recounted by Richard B. Moore in *Marcus Garvey and the Vision of Africa*:

> [On October 16, 1919,] a former employee, George Tyler, demanded to see Garvey at his office. . . . As it was reported, when Garvey appeared Tyler accused the leader of swindling him out of a $25 debt, pulled a gun and opened fire; one bullet grazed Garvey's forehead and the next wounded him in the leg. It was further reported that Amy Ashwood, then secretary to Marcus Garvey and soon to be his first wife, rushed in front of Garvey and grappled with the assassin.
>
> In jail after his arrest, Tyler is said to have declared that he had been sent to get Garvey. Later it was reported that Tyler jumped to his death from a window while being taken through a corridor by prison guards. But here, disturbing questions arise in the thinking mind. Were not the circumstances surrounding Tyler's attack upon Garvey and the subsequent "suicide" very strange and decidedly suspicious? Was George Tyler actually "sent to get Garvey?" . . . [Some suspect that New York district attorney Edwin Kilroe paid Tyler to assassinate Garvey.]

of St. Louis surprised the male delegates by introducing a resolution calling for women to be granted important positions within the organization. Turner wanted women to be given more recognition on UNIA committees, to be appointed to the executive branch and diplomatic corps, and to be put in complete charge of women's auxiliaries. Finally, the resolution stated that women be given these powers "so that Negro women all over the world can function without restrictions from men."[67]

This resolution showed that the UNIA women were tired of being relegated to fund-raising activities, domestic duties, and other traditional roles. Although Garvey initially opposed the women's plan, especially the desire for appointment to diplomatic missions, the female delegates overrode his objections. While few men within the UNIA had the courage to oppose Garvey, the women soon prevailed and the resolution was adopted by the organization.

The Universal African Black Cross Nurses

After 1922, UNIA women were granted total control over the Universal African Motor Corps, a female auxiliary trained in military discipline and automobile driving and repair. Members of the motor corps dressed in military uniform and received military training. This unusual organization was the only women's paramilitary group in the United States.

Women also controlled the Universal African Black Cross Nurses, one of the organization's most prominent auxiliaries, established during the first UNIA convention in 1920. The Black Cross nurses, as they were known, eventually opened chapters throughout the United States, Central America, and the Caribbean. The group was modeled on the Red Cross, the prominent international relief organization, which at the time refused membership to blacks.

The nurses were part of the UNIA Office of the Surgeon General, directed by Dr. D.D. Lewis, a Nigerian native who also headed the Montreal division of the UNIA. It was the job of this office to provide preventive health and hygiene measures, maternity services, education about contagious diseases, and counseling for men who had experienced racially motivated beatings. The Surgeon General appointed Sarah Branch as president of the Universal African Black Cross Nurses.

After the group was founded, the Black Cross nurses performed community work and public health services in black neighborhoods, specializing in infant health and home care. They wore long white robes or green nursing uniforms and caps bearing a black cross insignia. The nurses were a familiar sight in many black communities and marched near the front of UNIA parades in Harlem. In 1920 a UNIA report described the Black Cross nurses in the parade:

> The Black Cross nurses . . . made a truly inspiring spectacle. Clad in their white costumes, with their flowing white caps and their black crosses, these beautiful women of a sorrowed and bleeding but determined race, thrilled us men with pride and devotion to the cause that will eventually send us the call to make the supreme sacrifice on the battle plains of our beloved Africa, where their banner inscription, "We mean to Aid Our Boys," will be realized in faithful and loving ministrations.[68]

UNIA women march in a parade in Harlem. Tired of being relegated to fundraising and traditional roles, they demanded a greater role in the organization.

Contrary to the typical Garveyite imaginative language about the battlefields of Africa, the Black Cross nurses filled many immediate, practical needs. In most regions of the United States black people were refused medical treatment by white doctors and white-owned hospitals. Even during World War I, sick and wounded black soldiers were allowed to die because white personnel refused to treat them, and black doctors and nurses were in short supply since they were refused admission to medical schools and health organizations.

"Fear and Sorrow"

While the Black Cross nurses were the most public face of women within the UNIA, Amy Jacques Garvey was laboring behind the scenes collecting Marcus Garvey's speeches and arti-

Black Cross nurses served poor black communities. Here, they march in a 1922 parade.

cles from the *Negro World* and editing them for the book *Philosophy and Opinions of Marcus Garvey*, published in 1923. In the preface of the book, Jacques Garvey explains her reasons for assembling the speeches into book form:

> I decided to publish this volume in order to give to the public an opportunity of studying and forming an opinion of [Marcus Garvey]; not from inflated and misleading newspaper and magazine articles, but from expressions of thoughts enunciated by him in [defense] of his oppressed and struggling race; so that by his own words he may be judged, and Negroes the world over may be informed and inspired, for truth, brought to light, forces conviction, and a state of conviction inspires action.[69]

As editor of *Philosophy and Opinions of Marcus Garvey*, Jacques Garvey marginally revised some of her husband's words and curbed his tendencies toward repetition and hyperbole. Her work had more than editorial purposes, however. At the time that she was working on the book, Garvey was under indictment by the federal government for mail fraud. The case was based on the way the UNIA sold Black Star Line stock through the mails and mishandled money from the sales. Some of the money raised to purchase ships had apparently been wrongly used to pay for the printing of the *Negro World* and to shore up other UNIA businesses. Tens of thousands of dollars were simply unaccounted for. Fearing her husband's words would be used against him during his trial, Jacques Garvey removed some of his most provocative statements from the book, including portions of speeches discussing black armed rebellion and retribution against white colonialists in Africa.

After a lengthy trial, Garvey was convicted on one count of sending false promotional materials through the mail. He was sentenced to the maximum five years in prison and was immediately taken to New York's Tombs Penitentiary to await an appeal for a new trial. In the months that followed, the UNIA and Black Star Line organization fell into chaos. Workers who were fearful that they would also be indicted turned on one another, with some offering information to the government in exchange for

Amy Jacques Garvey, pictured in this rare but damaged photo, tried to keep her husband's movement alive while he was in prison.

clemency. After receiving death threats, Jacques Garvey began carrying a gun. Recalling that period, Jacques Garvey says "fear and sorrow now became [my] constant companions."[70]

Editing the *Negro World*

With Garvey in prison, Jacques Garvey worked tirelessly to keep the UNIA operating while trying to secure the release of her husband. Finally, in September 1923, she was able to convince a judge to free Garvey after providing a fifteen-thousand-dollar bail that had been cobbled together from small contributions by UNIA members.

Garvey's chronic asthma had been aggravated by his time in prison, so on October 1923 he and his wife decided to travel to a warmer climate to improve his health. While the couple made their way to the West Coast, Jacques Garvey began writing weekly articles for the *Negro World* describing the poverty, segregation, and hopelessness faced by most black people in the Midwest and the West. She discussed the rise of the Ku Klux Klan in Indiana, wrote of being refused service at a soda fountain in St. Louis, and analyzed the racial hatred she found in Los Angeles.

In keeping with the Pan-African themes put forward by the UNIA, Jacques Garvey explained that racism was such a problem in the United States that black people should not even attempt to change it. Instead, she wrote, it made more sense to "turn our eyes in the other direction and look towards Mother Africa, where we will be able to rise to the heights of true manhood and womanhood and live in happiness and prosperity with our brothers and sisters over there."[71]

Jacques Garvey's travel articles led her to assume the paper's editorial reins. On February 2, 1924, she began editing a page in the *Negro World* called "Our Women and What They Think." The page solicited opinion articles from female UNIA members and also featured a weekly editorial by Jacques Garvey.

One year to the day that Jacques Garvey took on the role of editor, Marcus Garvey's appeal was rejected by the New York Supreme Court. He was arrested and taken to a federal penitentiary in Atlanta, Georgia, where he remained until he was released for health reasons on November 27, 1927.

"Powerful Language"

During the time her husband was imprisoned, Jacques Garvey's editorials continued to promote the black nationalist messages that Marcus Garvey had refined over the years. She also added a female perspective, writing about the roles of black women in the home, in society, and during the struggle for civil rights. Like her husband, Jacques Garvey rarely minced words. As Jinx Coleman Broussard writes in *Giving a Voice to the Voiceless: Four Pioneering Black Women Journalists:*

> [She] not only revealed what she termed instances of white domination and oppression, but she sought to arouse in blacks [the] zeal to turn to themselves for their salvation. Her writings on race were laden with powerful language that denounced whites. She stridently chastised blacks as she sought to motivate them to take charge of their lives.[72]

One of the ways Jacques Garvey motivated people to take control was through economic gain, a consistent theme of the *Negro World*. Commenting on the need for black people to build successful businesses, Jacques Garvey tied economic profit to the Pan-African message, writing in 1925:

> It is imperative that the Negro create his own job, or face unemployment and consequently starvation. The black

"We Are Women of the Newer Type"

When Amy Jacques Garvey edited the page called "Our Women and What They Think" in the *Negro World*, she solicited comments from female UNIA members across the country. The following April 1924 letter from Eunice Lewis of Chicago, reprinted in volume five of *The Marcus Garvey and Universal Negro Improvement Association Papers*, demonstrates a feminist viewpoint:

> There are many people who think that a woman's place is only in the home—to raise children, cook, wash, and attend to the domestic affairs of the house. This idea, however, does not hold true with the New Negro Woman. The true type of the New Negro Woman . . . knows that in order to be a regular help to her race, it is necessary to learn all of the essentials of leadership. . . . Here are a few of the important places which the New Negro Woman desires to take in the rebirth of Africa, at home and abroad:
>
> 1. To work on par with men in the office as well as on the platform [stage].
>
> 2. To practice actual economy and thrift.
>
> 3. To teach practical and constructive race doctrine to the children.
>
> 4. To demand absolute respect from men of all races. . . .
>
> In a word, the New Negro Woman is revolutionizing the old type of male leadership. We are determined to have the Negro race represented and respected by every Negro leader.
>
> We are women of the newer type,
> Striving to make our Race sublime—
> Conscious that the time is ripe,
> To put our men on the firing line!

consumer is [deficient] unless he starts out immediately to produce [the] essentials of everyday life. . . . But the question of protection lies in the establishment of a government of his own in Africa strong enough to protect him in any part of the world he may reside.[73]

Jacques Garvey's attempts to spur her readers to action sometimes took a sarcastic and harshly critical tone. In an October 1926 editorial, for example, she castigated black workers: "The opportunities for doing business [do] not interest him; the light of slavery being still on him, he is afraid of responsibilities and clings to the idea of working under a white man and saying, 'Thank you boss' for a pay envelope, no matter how small it is. That's the reason why the race is so poor and backward."[74] The answer to such backwardness, according to Jacques Garvey, was to study the teachings of Marcus Garvey while generously supporting his beliefs, his plans, and his programs. By continuously promoting the UNIA movement while Garvey was in prison, Jacques Garvey was responsible for keeping the organization alive during very troubled times.

"Emancipated and Educated"

Perhaps it is no surprise that Jacques Garvey sounded much like Marcus Garvey when writing about black self-determination, white exploitation, economic independence, Pan-Africanism, racial solidarity, and international affairs. As a member of the UNIA and Garvey's personal secretary since she was nineteen years old, Jacques Garvey had been exposed to UNIA doctrine for years. However, when it came to gender issues Jacques Garvey departed from her husband's teachings. She believed that black women were superior to black men and, according to Broussard, "her editorials often praised black women while denigrating black men for not doing enough for their wives, children, and race."[75]

Jacques Garvey also advanced ideas that would be labeled feminist in later decades. As she wrote in December 1925, in some segments of society women were being "emancipated and educated to the point where they no longer consider themselves human incubators, and slaves to do the bidding of their husbands, but intelligent, independent human beings that assert and maintain their rights in co-partnership with their men."[76]

When editorializing about this co-partnership, Jacques Garvey echoed the advice that her husband generally aimed toward black men, telling women that they needed to become financially self-sufficient in terms of an ideal black woman:

She agitates for equal opportunities and gets them; she makes good on the job and gains the respect of men who heretofore opposed her. She prefers to be a bread-winner [rather] than a half-starved wife at home. She is not afraid of hard work, and by being independent, she gets more out of the present-day husband than her grandmother did in the good old days.[77]

"She . . . Beseeched, Chastised, Encouraged, Demanded"

Two days after Marcus Garvey was released from prison in 1927, Jacques Garvey penned her last column for the *Negro World*. During the years that she had been editor, she wrote more than 150 editorials. In her own passionate style, Broussard writes, "She crafted messages that beseeched, chastised, encouraged, demanded—and almost willed—that blacks worldwide act in their race's interest and rely on themselves to achieve racial freedom."[78]

While advocating independence and feminist causes, Jacques Garvey remained thoroughly dedicated to her husband. Upon his release from prison, he was immediately deported to Jamaica. Jacques Garvey returned to Jamaica with him, and they later toured England, France, and Germany. Both continued to contribute to the *Negro World*, but neither Garvey nor his newspaper regained its former influential status.

Like many other women in the UNIA, Amy Jacques Garvey was willing to fight and sacrifice for the black nationalist cause. Without her contributions, and those of thousands of UNIA women, the organization undoubtedly would have been less successful in promoting a message of black pride and self-reliance.

Chapter Six

The Fall of Garvey and the UNIA

Though the UNIA ultimately fell through its own naivete and mismanagement, from the very beginning it had drawn the scrutiny of powerful opponents in the government. The some-times inflammatory and revolutionary words of Marcus Garvey antagonized white politicians and law enforcement officials in the United States, Europe, the West Indies, and Africa, few if any of whom were willing to let the UNIA control the destinies of the black race.

Garvey also never gained the valuable support of black lead-ers such as W.E.B. Du Bois and his colleagues in the NAACP, who looked on Garvey as little more than a crook, a Jamaican rabble-rouser, and an eccentric who dressed ostentatiously as an admiral while collecting large sums of money from gullible supporters. Garvey's message of black nationalism and segrega-tion was abhorrent to those fighting for acceptance by white society.

Importantly, the UNIA was fractured by dissent and dishon-esty within its own ranks. Some members of the organization stole money, and others informed authorities in order to foil the group's plans. For example, after an altercation with Garvey, the first president of the New York UNIA chapter, Samuel Duncan, wrote a letter to British authorities stating that Garvey was "a dangerous Negro agitator who desired to stir up hatred between colored people and white people."[79] Duncan recommended that the British government deny ships from the Black Star Line entry into its European and colonial ports. While it is unknown whether British authorities were acting on Duncan's recommendations, they did as he suggested and the financial prospects of the Black Star Line were seriously hamstrung. Such machinations caused Garvey to write in 1930, "There is no doubt that the Negro is his own greatest enemy. He is jealous of himself, envious and covetous. . . . This I know was responsible for the collapse of the Black Star Line."[80]

Garvey, too, was at times his own worst enemy. In his heedless pursuit of the dream of black independence, he ignored standard business practices and even common sense. From the mishandling of the Black Star Line investors' money to the purchase of ships that were barely seaworthy, Garvey ignored the advice of experienced professionals. In a rush to garner good publicity he often made impulsive decisions that were financially questionable.

Garvey and the Ku Klux Klan

It was Garvey's poor handling of financial affairs that eventually landed him in prison. However, no decision hurt his public image more than his earlier meeting with Edward Young Clarke, an advertising executive in Louisiana who was the imperial wizard of the Ku Klux Klan. Clarke preached an anti-black, anti-Semitic, and anti-Catholic doctrine and was responsible for transforming the Klan from an isolated southern hate group into a national organization with more than 1 million members. In Klan parlance, Clarke was known as the head Kleagle, a title given to KKK recruiters.

Clarke requested a meeting with Garvey on June 25, 1922, in Atlanta. Garvey was in the midst of an extensive lecture tour of the United States following the collapse of the Black Star Line. At the time, UNIA members in the South were facing arrest and even lynching simply for supporting the organization. Garvey did not help the situation there, making incendiary statements that startled and angered his followers and emboldened his enemies. For

Garvey believed that the KKK, pictured here in a nighttime gathering, represented the white majority viewpoint.

example, at a speech in Raleigh, North Carolina, Garvey praised white violence for having created a desperate situation for blacks that "lynched racial pride into the Negroes." He also reinforced racist clichés when talking about a mass movement of black people to Africa, saying "[I do] not want all [Negroes] to go over there. . . . No there are lots of lazy Negroes who we don't want over there. You just stay here where it suits you."[81]

In New Orleans, Garvey continued to shock, accepting Jim Crow laws as a way of selling his audience on the idea that they should move to Africa:

> This is a white man's country. He found it, he conquered it and we can't blame him because he wants to keep it. I'm not vexed with the white man of the South for Jim Crowing me because I'm black.

I never built any street cars or railroads. The white man built them for your own convenience. And if I don't want to ride where he's willing to let me then I'd better walk.[82]

Such statements ignored the fact that most southern railroads had originally been built by black slave labor. However, the words got Clarke's attention, and he then called for the meeting with Garvey. At the time, the Klan was under investigation by federal authorities, and Clarke was trying to change the image of the

"I Admire the Ku Klux Klan for Its Honesty"

Marcus Garvey believed that the Ku Klux Klan's racist beliefs were simply representational of the majority viewpoint of white America. In a February 1923 speech at Liberty Hall, printed in volume five of *The Marcus Garvey and Universal Negro Improvement Association Papers*, Garvey explains his thoughts on the KKK:

I admire the Ku Klux Klan for its honesty of intention in expressing to the people what it means; and I have more regard for the Ku Klux Klan . . . than all the other white people in America, because they feel the same way but are not honest enough to tell us what they mean. The man who is going to give you a licking and who prepares you for that licking is a better friend of yours than the fellow who is going to give you a licking that you know nothing about until he gives it to you.

I have the highest regard for . . . the Ku Klux Klan for telling me openly and telling 15,000,000 of us openly: "Negroes, we stand for white supremacy. We are not going to give you a chance to be our social, political or economic equals. If you have sense you will go out and look out for yourselves." So . . . I have nothing to do with the Ku Klux Klan more than thanking them for the information that they have given to me, because as they . . . stand for white supremacy, so will 400,000,0000 Negroes, under the leadership of the Red, the Black and the Green [UNIA flag], stand . . . for black supremacy.

KKK from one of a violent vigilante organization to one of a powerful political party based on white separatism. Clarke hoped the publicity generated by the meeting would help burnish the image of the Klan, showing it as peacefully supporting the Pan-African movement as a way of easing racial tensions in the South.

For his part, Garvey looked at the conference as something of a peace summit between two powerful enemies. He needed the Klan's tacit support in order for the UNIA to grow in the South. In his book *Race First: The Ideological and Organizational Struggles of Marcus Garvey and the Universal Negro Improvement Association*, Tony Martin describes what took place during the two-hour meeting:

> Clarke emphasized that America was a white man's country, that his organization stood for racial purity, and denied that the Klan was responsible for all the incidents of racial intolerance attributed to it. Garvey outlined the UNIA's philosophy. . . . As a result of the discussions Clarke expressed sympathy for the aims of the UNIA, while Garvey was reinforced in his suspicion that the Klan represented the invisible government of the United States. He became convinced that this organization represented the white American majority viewpoint. . . . Garvey seems to have gotten an assurance from Clarke that the Klan would refrain from harassing the UNIA. . . . The end result of all this was that Garvey concluded that it would henceforth be more worthwhile to push forward with the UNIA program to build a strong government in Africa . . . rather than waste time attacking the Klan.[83]

"Garvey Must Go"

The meeting was a public relations disaster, and Garvey returned to New York for the August UNIA convention to face harsh criticism. William Pickens of the NAACP did not think it was wise for black people to surrender the United States to the white race, telling Garvey, "You say in effect to the Ku Klux Klan: All right! Give us Africa and we in turn concede you America as 'white man's country.' In that you make a poor deal; for twelve million people you give up EVERYTHING and in exchange get NOTHING."[84]

A. Philip Randolph denounced Garvey as a "messenger boy" of the Klan.

Civil rights leader and Socialist agitator A. Philip Randolph used his newspaper, the *Messenger*, to denounce Garvey in bold headlines that read: "MARCUS GARVEY! THE BLACK IMPERIAL WIZARD BECOMES MESSENGER BOY OF THE WHITE KU KLUX KLEAGLE." In the accompanying article, Randolph claimed his organization, the Friends of Negro Freedom, would "drive Garvey and Garveyism in all its sinister viciousness from the American soil."[85]

In September, Chandler Owen, another member of the Friends of Negro Freedom, wrote an article in the *Messenger* entitled "Should Marcus Garvey Be Deported?":

The die is cast, Marcus Garvey *must* go. Every self-respecting Negro is called upon to rescue the race from the Black Kluxer's disgrace. Garvey must get out of Negro life everywhere. There is no place in America for a black race baiter, one time reviling all white men; and a "good nigger" race traitor, at another time selling out the rights of all Negroes.[86]

In early 1923, Owen, Pickens, and others continued their campaign against Garvey by sending a long letter to U.S. attorney general Harry Daugherty calling Garvey an "unscrupulous demagogue" who sought to "spread among Negroes distrust and hatred of all white people." The letter warned that the UNIA was populated by "ministers without churches, physicians without patients, lawyers without clients . . . [and] Negro sharks and ignorant Negro fanatics."[87] The letter went on to list alleged acts of violence committed by UNIA members against opponents of the organization. The writers concluded by saying that they were only sounding a warning because of "the gathering storm of race prejudice and the sense of imminent menace of this insidious movement which, cancer-like, is gnawing at the very vitals of peace and safety—of civic harmony and inter-racial accord."[88]

"A Fixation on Garvey"

Unbeknownst to the letter writers, the attorney general was well aware of the activities of Marcus Garvey. Various Bureau of Investigation, State Department, and military investigators had been scrutinizing Garvey's activities for several years. Military intelligence and the State Department were concerned with Garvey's newspaper, the *Negro World*, and its radicalizing effect on black laborers working for American-owned fruit, shipping, and coffee companies in Central and South America. The Bureau of Investigation was troubled by Garvey's call for black nationalism and the possible race war that would be necessary for black people to achieve independence. The U.S. postmaster general expressed concern that Garvey's charismatic leadership was attracting hundreds of thousands of followers worldwide while allowing the UNIA to raise large sums of money through the mail. The sale of stock through the Black Star Line was particularly disturbing to postal official Roger A. Bowen, who believed that the *Negro World* contained objectionable content and was thus in violation of U.S. postal laws. He was in favor of suspending the UNIA's second-class mailing permit. No action could be taken, however, until Garvey was formally convicted of criminal charges.

Bowen convinced the Bureau of Investigation to begin monitoring Garvey, the UNIA, and the *Negro World*, telling investigators that the flamboyant Garvey tended "to instill into the minds of negroes . . . that they have been greatly wronged and oppressed by the white races and that they can only hope for relief and redress through concerted and aggressive action on their part."[89]

At the time, J. Edgar Hoover was the head of a new section of the Bureau of Investigation that scrutinized Communist, Socialist, and civil rights groups deemed radical by government

The Garvey-Must-Go Campaign

As early as 1920 Marcus Garvey was under fire by A. Philip Randolph and Chandler Owen. These men and other prominent black leaders organized the Garvey-Must-Go campaign, explained on the Public Broadcasting Services Web site:

A. Philip Randolph and other black leaders . . . derided Garvey's proposed solutions for the problems of African Americans. They believed that his plans for black progress, including the Black Star Line and the establishment of a pan-African empire, were unrealistic and ill-advised; they considered the Universal Negro Improvement Association's grandiose titles and military regalia to be preposterous; and they thought Garvey, with his assumption of a regal posture under the title "Provisional President of Africa," to be little more than a self-aggrandizing buffoon. A. Philip Randolph, who had introduced Garvey to his first American audience on a Harlem street corner, said Garvey had "succeeded in making the Negro the laughingstock of the world." . . .

Black opposition to Garvey coalesced into what came to be known as the Garvey-Must-Go campaign. Supporters of the campaign, known collectively as the Friends of Negro Freedom, intended to unmask Garvey as a fraud before his black supporters. They also appealed to the federal government to step up investigations of irregularities in the Black Star Line, and to look into alleged acts of violence on the part of Garvey's inner circle.

MARCUS GARVEY MUST GO!

Four of the Greatest Negro Meetings Ever Held in New York,

Sundays — August 6th, 13th, 20th and 27th

SHUFFLE INN MUSIC PARLORS

A flyer calls for Marcus Garvey's ouster.

officials. In 1919 race riots were erupting across America in Chicago, Norfolk, Omaha, and elsewhere, and Hoover was convinced that Garvey's words were partly to blame for the agitation. The UNIA leader quickly became Hoover's number-one target, according to Theodore Kornweibel Jr.: "Hoover and the

Justice Department were clearly hooked on a fixation on Garvey which would before long become a vendetta."[90]

As Hoover began the investigation into Garvey, his plan was to find solid evidence of mail fraud concerning the Black Star Line. If Garvey was convicted, the government could deport him. When the investigation began, however, Hoover seemed disappointed, writing, "Unfortunately . . . he has not as yet violated any federal law whereby he could be proceeded against on the grounds of being an undesirable alien, from the point of view of deportation."[91]

Hoover utilized the resources of at least seven federal agencies to dig up enough evidence to arrest Garvey. Meanwhile, black undercover agents were hired to infiltrate the offices of the UNIA. The first, James Wormley Jones, a veteran of World War I and a former Washington, D.C., detective, was given the code number "800." Jones quickly rose through the UNIA ranks, and by the summer of 1920 he was reviewing financial statements of the organization's Harlem restaurant, registering incoming mail, and monitoring the mail for sales of Black Star Line stock.

Deputies escort a handcuffed Marcus Garvey to prison after his sentencing for mail fraud.

By January 1922 Jones had gathered enough evidence to indict Garvey for using the mail to defraud buyers of Black Star Line stock. After his conviction, many Garvey supporters felt that he was singled out for prosecution by Hoover, who would stop at nothing to jail their leader. Garvey's enemies in the Garvey-Must-Go group felt vindicated. Whether or not the UNIA leader was a swindler or simply an inexperienced and naive businessman has remained a long-standing debate. However, as Kornweibel writes, "The Justice Department found Garvey's vulnerability in his chaotic business practices. . . . What is undeniable is that hundreds of thousands of dollars of Black Star Line stockholders' money were squandered and misappropriated. For this Garvey had to bear major responsibility, and in the end he paid dearly."[92]

Deported to Jamaica

By February 1925, when Garvey was incarcerated in the federal penitentiary in Atlanta, his only assets were forty dollars and several hundred shares of worthless Black Star Line stock. Largely through Amy Jacques Garvey's efforts, however, many of her husband's supporters remained loyal. From UNIA branches across the globe, members sent petitions, telegrams, letters, and resolutions to U.S. government officials. In cities across the nation, the UNIA organized mass rallies where protesters demanded Garvey be freed without deportation. Black churches in Harlem often celebrated "Marcus Garvey Sunday," during which prayer meetings were held for the imprisoned UNIA leader. Black and white newspaper reporters investigated the government's role in and tactics during Garvey's trial and found many irregularities. For example, the judge, Julian Mack, was a member of the NAACP, an organization that long opposed Garvey.

The pleas for clemency grew until President Calvin Coolidge finally commuted Garvey's sentence on November 18, 1927. Coolidge's exact motives are uncertain. Historians believe that it was not injustice in the sentence but rather Garvey's poor health that motivated the president to free him. Garvey suffered from bronchitis and asthma attacks and spent a great deal of time in the prison hospital. Officials feared Garvey would die in prison and become a martyr to the Pan-African movement, so they freed him and deported him immediately to Jamaica.

Back in the land of his birth, Garvey was treated to a hero's welcome. He settled down with his wife, and the couple had two sons. In the following years Garvey supported his family working at a real estate office, an amusement park, a collection agency, and a newspaper. He also formed a political party in Jamaica and ran unsuccessfully for a seat in the Legislative Council.

In April 1928 Garvey traveled to Great Britain, hoping to revive the UNIA, but a speech booked at the famous Royal Albert Hall was sparsely attended and drew little attention. Meanwhile, in the United States another factor served to diminish the role of the UNIA. Garvey's trial had been closely covered in newspapers throughout the nation, and white society took notice. African Americans who were known to be members of the UNIA were often fired from their jobs or harassed by local authorities. Without Garvey's charismatic leadership, hundreds of thousands of people let their membership in the UNIA lapse.

Last Days in Obscurity

In 1929 the stock market crashed and a worldwide economic depression began. Over the next decade, U.S. unemployment rose to 30 percent, and millions of whites and blacks alike lost their jobs. Harlem's relative prosperity came to an abrupt end as the dream of achieving equality with white society was dashed in the dire economic climate of the Great Depression.

Meanwhile, the few remaining members of the UNIA movement splintered into two groups. At a 1929 convention in Kingston, Garvey presided over the newly incorporated UNIA and African Communities League of the World. In New York, a rival organization, UNIA, Incorporated, was founded by Fred A. Toote, a clergyman in the African Orthodox Church. Toote's move was denounced in the *Negro World*, still controlled by Garvey loyalists until it went out of business in July 1932.

In the Depression years of the 1930s, Garvey struggled in obscurity. In 1934 he attempted to revive the UNIA with a Kingston convention. In sharp contrast to the crowds attending the conventions of the early 1920s, Garvey's final UNIA conference attracted ten Americans and twenty-five others from the West Indies and Central America. Sick from asthma and heart disease, and disheartened by his failures, Garvey moved alone to London in 1935. He attempted to preach to crowds in Hyde Park but was mercilessly heckled there. George Padmore, a columnist for the *Chicago Defender*, described Garvey at this time as "vain, arrogant, and highly sensitive to criticism."[93]

In January 1940 Garvey suffered a stroke and was incapacitated. In the United States a rumor spread that the former UNIA leader had died. In May, acting on this rumor, the *Defender* published Garvey's obituary. On June 9, the story goes, Garvey was given a copy of the *Defender.* Upon reading his own obituary, Garvey gave a loud groan and fell to the floor, suffering a second stroke. The next morning he was dead. Jacques Garvey continued the struggle for black nationalism, editing the *African*, a journal published in Harlem in the 1940s. In 1963 she published *Garvey and Garveyism*, and she later published two collections of essays, *Black Power in America* and *The Impact of Garvey in Africa and Jamaica.* She died in 1973.

"The UNIA . . . Hasn't Started to Live"

At the time of Marcus Garvey's death, the Pan-African movement had also suffered a decline in popularity. Ironically, the death of its leading proponent helped to revive the organization. On July 1, 1940, Garvey was honored by hundreds of people in Harlem at a public meeting. On August 17, 1945, in honor of Garvey's birthday, the UNIA sponsored an international conference in Harlem where dozens of delegates from the West Indies, Africa, and the United States gave speeches.

In 1937 Garvey had predicted that the movement he founded would continue. He told an audience in Toronto, "Those of you who thought the UNIA was dead or is dead have made a terrible mistake. It hasn't started to live in its reality."[94] His words proved prophetic in ways he never imagined. Although he died in obscurity, he was remembered as a hero and visionary during the civil rights movement of the 1960s and was

By 1936, when this photograph was taken, Marcus Garvey had lost most of his following.

The UNIA Today

■

Membership in the Universal Negro Improvement Association and African Communities League dwindled to less than one hundred after Garvey's death, but the organization has been revived today in name and in honor of Garvey's ideals. The mission of the modern UNIA is expressed on the organization's official Web site:

> As U.N.I.A. and A.C.I. members, we are Garveyites. Garveyites realize that race and color play an important part in the world today. We realize that the coming into being of a powerful African nation will mean the easing of the color bar wherever African people live. . . . Garveyites have been taught that freedom can only be firmly established in consecrated soil. It must be sown deep in belief in one's self, and in one's own ability to conquer adversity. Freedom is carved out of dreams of greatness, and a determination to turn those dreams into living realities. It is planted in a common longing to shape one's own fate. . . .
>
> We believe God created all women and men equal, that he gave us all the ingredients of greatness. What one race can do, all others may accomplish. . . .
>
> Until we prove to the world, that we too, are women and men capable of doing what other men and women have done, we will always be looked upon as a little less than other women and men. Only when we too have created states, built nations, and created the governments comparable to those of the modern men and women, will we be able to erase the stigma of inferiority.

honored as the first to popularize the notions of black pride and black nationalism. Although he was beset on all sides by political enemies, inept managers, and financial disasters, no one could doubt that Marcus Garvey was a zealous believer in the Pan-African ideal. And that message was able to endure long after the movement's greatest proponent was gone.

Garvey's Legacy and the Black Power Movement

Marcus Garvey was one of the most famous and controversial black men in the world from the middle of 1918 until his imprisonment in early 1925. In less than seven years the Jamaican immigrant rose from obscurity, tapped into the widespread anger and resentment of African Americans against racism, and offered solutions that seemed workable to many. For a time he was the leading spokesman for black Americans and a hero and prophet to millions around the world.

Perhaps Garvey's questionable business practices, outsized ego, and ill health would have ended his days in the limelight even without federal intervention. There is little doubt, however, that aggressive investigation into his organization and affairs hastened his downfall and diminished his role as spokesman for the black race. As Theodore Kornweibel Jr. writes, "The Bureau [of Investigation] and its federal intelligence partners watched Garvey, combed his speeches for seditious utterances, monitored his private life, infiltrated his organization, broke into his offices, and brought him to trial, conviction, imprisonment, and deportation."[95]

While J. Edgar Hoover, having neutralized the UNIA leader, might have been satisfied with his work, he would live to see Garveyism revived once again in the 1960s. This time the message of black pride and self-determination would prove unstoppable and would change the face of the United States and the world. Amy Jacques Garvey explains when she says that her "husband was forerunner of the 'Black Power' and 'Black is Beautiful'"[96] movements popular in the late 1960s and early 1970s.

Malcolm X and Marcus Garvey pins displayed for sale in Harlem in the 1990s recall Garvey's influence on later civil rights leaders.

Visitors pay their respects at the tomb of Marcus Garvey, a man who is credited with fueling community activism and black nationalism.

Historical records back up Jacques Garvey's claim. The term *black power* was coined in 1966 by Stokley Carmichael, the chairman of the civil rights group Student Nonviolent Coordinating Committee (SNCC). According to a SNCC policy statement of that time, "[Black power] is a call for black people in this country to unite, to recognize their heritage, to build a sense of community. It is a call for black people to begin to define their own goals, to lead their own organizations, and to support those organizations."[97]

Marcus Garvey uttered such sentiments countless times between 1914 and 1940, and there is little doubt that the UNIA leader influenced many renowned civil rights leaders of the 1950s and 1960s. Elijah Mohammed, who led the influential Nation of Islam, or Black Muslim organization, from 1934 to 1975 was a corporal in the Chicago division of the UNIA in the 1920s. Another prominent Nation of Islam leader, Malcolm X, was greatly influenced by Garveyism and the UNIA message. His father was the vice president of the Detroit division, and his West

Indian mother was a member of the UNIA. In 1964 Malcolm X spoke about the influence of Marcus Garvey on the civil rights movement of the 1950s and 1960s:

> It was Marcus Garvey's philosophy of Pan Africanism that initiated the entire freedom movement. . . . All the freedom movements that are taking place right here in America today were initiated by the work and teachings of Marcus Garvey. The entire Black Muslim philosophy here in America is feeding upon the seeds that were planted by Marcus Garvey.[98]

Garvey also had a profound influence on Martin Luther King Jr., who led the American civil rights movement from 1955 until his death in 1968. King, more than any other African American leader, has been credited with uniting African Americans in the struggle against racism, prejudice, and segregation. Yet when King laid a wreath on the Marcus Garvey shrine in Jamaica in June 1965, he gave credit to the man who founded a movement dedicated to black equality:

> Marcus Garvey was the first man of color in the history of the United States to lead and develop a mass movement. He was the first man, on a mass scale and level, to give millions of Negroes a sense of dignity and destiny, and make the Negro feel that he was somebody. . . . Marcus Garvey . . . gave to the millions of Negroes in the United States a sense of personhood, a sense of manhood, and a sense of somebodiness.[99]

Historians of the black civil rights movement credit Garvey for his pivotal role in the rise of community activism and black nationalism, two of the most distinctive aspects of the movement. Indeed, the red, black, and green flag introduced by Garvey to represent the UNIA became a prominent black nationalist symbol, incorporated into a number of African national flags during the era of African independence. Although he would never live to see African Americans at the head of corporations, in high public office, and as members of the Supreme Court, there is little doubt that Garvey's rabble-rousing career jump-started a movement that would permanently change American society.

Notes

Introduction:
A Controversial Man Leads
a Controversial Movement

1. Quoted in Tony Martin, *Race First: The Ideological and Organizational Struggles of Marcus Garvey and the Universal Negro Improvement Association*. Dover, MA: Majority, 1986, p. 6.
2. Quoted in Judith Stein, *The World of Marcus Garvey: Race and Class in Modern Society*. Baton Rouge: Louisiana State University Press, 1986, p. 1.

Chapter 1: Racial Oppression and Violence in Jim Crow America

3. Leon Litwack, *Trouble in Mind: Black Southerners in the Age of Jim Crow*. New York: Alfred A. Knopf, 1998, p. xiv.
4. Quoted in Allen Weinstein and Frank Otto Gatell, eds., *The Segregation Era, 1863–1954: A Modern Reader*. New York: Oxford University Press, 1970, p. 131.
5. Quoted in Litwack, *Trouble in Mind*, p. 289.
6. Quoted in Litwack, *Trouble in Mind*, p. 290.
7. Quoted in Litwack, *Trouble in Mind*, p. 288.
8. Quoted in Litwack, *Trouble in Mind*, p. 482.

9. Allan H. Spear, *Black Chicago: The Making of a Negro Ghetto, 1890–1920*. Chicago: University of Chicago Press, 1967, p. 168.
10. Quoted in Alain Locke, ed., *The New Negro: An Interpretation*. New York: Arno, 1968, p. 305.
11. Locke, *The New Negro*, p. 3.
12. Quoted in Locke, *The New Negro*, p. 301.
13. *New York Age*, "Old Fifteenth Given Rousing Reception," February 22, 1919.
14. Quoted in African Studies Center, "American Series Introduction: Volume I: 1826–August 1919," The Marcus Garvey and Universal Negro Improvement Association Papers Project, 2005. www.international. ucla.edu/africa/mgpp/.

Chapter 2: A New Black Moses

15. Quoted in John Henrik Clarke, ed., *Marcus Garvey and the Vision of Africa*. New York: Random House, 1974, p. 73.
16. Quoted in Amy Jacques Garvey, *Garvey and Garveyism*. New York: Octagon, 1978, p. 11.
17. Quoted in Clarke, ed., *Marcus Garvey and the Vision of Africa*, p. 74.
18. Garvey, *Garvey and Garveyism*, p. 8.
19. Quoted in Clarke, ed., *Marcus Garvey and the Vision of Africa*, p. 75.

20. Garvey, *Garvey and Garveyism*, p. 15.

21. Quoted in Herbert Aptheker et al., eds., *The Marcus Garvey and Universal Negro Improvement Association Papers*, vol. 1. Berkeley and Los Angeles: University of California Press, 1983, p. 213.

22. Quoted in Aptheker et al., eds., *The Marcus Garvey and Universal Negro Improvement Association Papers*, vol. 1, p. 246.

23. Imanuel Geiss, *The Pan-African Movement: A History of Pan-Africanism in America, Europe, and Africa*. New York, Africana, 1974, p. 267.

24. Quoted in Robert A. Hill, ed., *Marcus Garvey, Life and Lessons: A Centennial Companion to the Marcus Garvey and Universal Negro Improvement Association Papers*. Berkeley and Los Angeles: University of California Press, 1987, p. 37.

25. Roi Ottley, *New World-A-Coming*. New York: Arno, 1968, pp. 69–70.

26. Quoted in Aptheker et al., eds., *The Marcus Garvey and Universal Negro Improvement Association Papers*, vol. 1, pp. lxxviii–lxxxix.

27. Quoted in Aptheker et al., eds., *The Marcus Garvey and Universal Negro Improvement Association Papers*, vol. 1, p. lxxxix.

28. Quoted in Aptheker et al., eds., *The Marcus Garvey and Universal Negro Improvement Association Papers*, vol. 1, p. 244.

Chapter 3: Spreading the Pan-African Message

29. Quoted in Martin, *Race First*, p. 44.

30. Quoted in Aptheker et al., eds., *The Marcus Garvey and Universal Negro Improvement Association Papers*, vol. 2, p. 491.

31. Quoted in Aptheker et al., eds., *The Marcus Garvey and Universal Negro Improvement Association Papers*, vol. 2, p. 493.

32. Quoted in Milfred C. Fierce, *The Pan-African Idea in the United States, 1900–1919*. New York: Garland, 1993, p. 3.

33. Quoted in Fierce, *The Pan-African Idea in the United States*, p. 7.

34. Fierce, *The Pan-African Idea in the United States*, p. 38.

35. Quoted in Aptheker et al., eds., *The Marcus Garvey and Universal Negro Improvement Association Papers*, vol. 2, p. 559.

36. Quoted in Stein, *The World of Marcus Garvey*, p. 109.

37. Quoted in Aptheker et al., eds., *The Marcus Garvey and Universal Negro Improvement Association Papers*, vol. 2, p. 667.

38. Quoted in Aptheker et al., eds., *The Marcus Garvey and Universal Negro Improvement Association Papers*, vol. 2, p. 671.

39. Quoted in Aptheker et al., eds., *The Marcus Garvey and Universal Negro Improvement Association Papers*, vol. 2, p. 668.

40. Quoted in Aptheker et al., eds., *The Marcus Garvey and Universal Negro Improvement Association Papers*, vol. 2, p. 571.

41. Quoted in Martin, *Race First*, p. 45.

42. Quoted in Martin, *Race First*, p. 48.
43. Quoted in Martin, *Race First*, p. 48.
44. Quoted in Martin, *Race First*, p. 90.
45. Quoted in Aptheker et al., eds., *The Marcus Garvey and Universal Negro Improvement Association Papers*, vol. 2, p. 560.
46. Quoted in Wilson Jeremiah Moses, *Creative Conflict in African American Thought.* Cambridge, UK: Cambridge University Press, 2004, p. 250.

Chapter 4: The UNIA Mission: Black Enterprise and African Nationhood

47. Quoted in Theodore Kornweibel Jr., *Seeing Red: Federal Campaigns Against Black Militancy, 1919–1925.* Bloomington: Indiana University Press, 1998, p. 106.
48. Kornweibel, *Seeing Red*, p. 106.
49. Quoted in Stein, *The World of Marcus Garvey*, p. 64.
50. Quoted in Stein, *The World of Marcus Garvey*, pp. 69–70.
51. Lens Nembhard, *Trials and Triumphs of Marcus Garvey.* Millwood, NY: Kraus Reprint, 1978, p. 26.
52. Quoted in Elton C. Fax, *Garvey: The Story of a Pioneer Black Nationalist.* New York: Dodd, Mead, 1972, p. 102.
53. Fax, *Garvey*, p. 103.
54. Quoted in Clarke, ed., *Marcus Garvey and the Vision of Africa*, p. 131.
55. Hugh Mulzac, *A Star to Steer By.* New York: International, 1963, p. 87.
56. Quoted in Fax, *Garvey*, p. 107.
57. Quoted in Aptheker et al., eds., *The Marcus Garvey and Universal Negro Improvement Association Papers*, vol. 2, p. 297.
58. Quoted in Aptheker et al., eds., *The Marcus Garvey and Universal Negro Improvement Association Papers*, vol. 2, p. 372.
59. Quoted in Aptheker et al., eds., *The Marcus Garvey and Universal Negro Improvement Association Papers*, vol. 2, pp. 297–98.
60. Quoted in Martin, *Race First*, p. 37.

Chapter 5: Women Take the Leading Roles

61. Barbara Bair, "Online Forum: Comparing the Role of Women in the Garvey Movement," Public Broadcasting Service, 2000. www.pbs.org/wgbh/amex/garvey/sfeature/sf_forum_14.html.
62. Quoted in Ula Yvette Taylor, *The Veiled Garvey: The Life and Times of Amy Jacques Garvey.* Chapel Hill: University of North Carolina Press, 2002, p. 23.
63. Quoted in Lionel M. Yard, *Biography of Amy Ashwood Garvey, 1897–1969: Co-Founder of the UNIA.* Washington, DC: Associated, 1990, p. 14.
64. Taylor, *The Veiled Garvey*, p. 44.
65. Quoted in Taylor, *The Veiled Garvey*, p. 29.
66. Quoted in Taylor, *The Veiled Garvey*, p. 34.
67. Quoted in Taylor, *The Veiled Garvey*, p. 44.
68. Quoted in Aptheker et al., eds., *The Marcus Garvey and Universal Negro Improvement Association Papers*, vol. 1, p. 493.

69. Amy Jacques Garvey, ed., preface to *Philosophy and Opinions of Marcus Garvey*, by Marcus Garvey. New York: Atheneum, 1980.

70. Quoted in Taylor, *The Veiled Garvey*, p. 51.

71. Amy Jacques Garvey, "Mrs. Amy Jacques Garvey Writes of Her Interesting Experiences," *Negro World*, November 17, 1923, p. 2.

72. Jinx Coleman Broussard, *Giving a Voice to the Voiceless: Four Pioneering Black Women Journalists*. New York: Routledge, 2004, p. 109.

73. Quoted in Broussard, *Giving a Voice to the Voiceless*, pp. 117–18.

74. Amy Jacques Garvey, "Stop Hunting a Job and Create One," *Negro World*, October 9, 1926.

75. Broussard, *Giving a Voice to the Voiceless*, p. 124.

76. Amy Jacques Garvey, "Woman's Function in Life," *Negro World*, December 19, 1926.

77. Amy Jacques Garvey, "Women as Leaders Nationally and Racially," *Negro World*, October 24, 1925.

78. Broussard, *Giving a Voice to the Voiceless*, p. 132.

Chapter 6:
The Fall of Garvey and the UNIA

79. Quoted in Clarke, ed., *Marcus Garvey and the Vision of Africa*, p. 140.

80. Quoted in Clarke, ed., *Marcus Garvey and the Vision of Africa*, p. 141.

81. Quoted in Stein, *The World of Marcus Garvey*, p. 154.

82. Quoted in Fax, *Garvey*, p. 161.

83. Martin, *Race First*, pp. 345–46.

84. Quoted in Stein, *The World of Marcus Garvey*, p. 164.

85. Quoted in Stein, *The World of Marcus Garvey*, p. 161.

86. Quoted in Fax, *Garvey*, p. 164.

87. Quoted in Aptheker et al., eds., *The Marcus Garvey and Universal Negro Improvement Association Papers*, vol. 5, p. 183.

88. Quoted in Aptheker et al., eds., *The Marcus Garvey and Universal Negro Improvement Association Papers*, vol. 5, p. 186.

89. Quoted in Kornweibel, *Seeing Red*, p. 102.

90. Quoted in Public Broadcasting Service, "People & Events: J. Edgar Hoover," 2000. www.pbs.org/wgbh/amex/garvey/peopleevents/p_hoover.html.

91. Quoted in Kornweibel, *Seeing Red*, p. 105.

92. Kornweibel, *Seeing Red*, p. 129.

93. Quoted in Stein, *The World of Marcus Garvey*, p. 266.

94. Quoted in Clarke, ed., *Marcus Garvey and the Vision of Africa*, p. 339.

Epilogue: Garvey's Legacy and the Black Power Movement

95. Kornweibel, *Seeing Red*, p. 131.

96. Quoted in Clarke, ed., *Marcus Garvey and the Vision of Africa*, p. 373.

97. Quoted in Bettye Collier-Thomas and V.P. Franklin, eds., *Sisters in the Struggle*. New York: New York University Press, 2001, p. 198.

98. Quoted in Garvey, *Garvey and Garveyism*, pp. 307–308.

99. Quoted in Garvey, *Garvey and Garveyism*, p. 308.

For Further Reading

Books

Peggy Caravantes, *Marcus Garvey: Black Nationalist*. Greensboro: Morgan Reynolds, 2004. A biography of Garvey that covers his early years in Jamaica, his belief in race consciousness, his work in the United States, and other topics.

Ann Gaines, *The Harlem Renaissance in American History*. Berkeley Heights, NJ: Enslow, 2002. An exploration of African Americans in Harlem, New York, in the 1920s with a focus on music, theater, art, and literature.

Laban Carrick Hill, *Harlem Stomp! A Cultural History of the Harlem Renaissance*. This book discusses African American life, music, art, literature, and culture in New York City during the 1920s.

Sidney J. Lemelle, *Pan-Africanism for Beginners*. New York: Writers and Readers, 1992. A documentary comic book that explains the basic tenets of the Pan-African movement.

Anne Schraff, *Marcus Garvey: Controversial Champion of Black Pride*. Berkeley Heights, NJ: Enslow, 2004. This work chronicles the life of Marcus Garvey, the charismatic black leader who began a crusade for black people to fight against oppression.

Web Sites

The Marcus Garvey and Universal Negro Improvement Association Papers Project (www.international. ucla.edu/africa/mgpp). This site, hosted by the African Studies Center at the University of California, Los Angeles, features documents, speeches, photos, and audio selections of Garvey and the organization he founded.

Negro World (www.negroworld.com). An online edition of the newspaper Marcus Garvey founded in 1918. The site features old articles from Garvey and current news and opinions from today's international black leaders.

Universal Negro Improvement Association and African Communities League (www.unia-acl.org). The official site of the organization Marcus Garvey founded in Harlem in 1918.

Works Consulted

Books

Herbert Aptheker et al., eds., *The Marcus Garvey and Universal Negro Improvement Association Papers.* Vols. 1–5. Berkeley and Los Angeles: University of California Press, 1983. An extensive collection of writings, editorials, memoranda, speeches, and other documents concerning the UNIA and its leader written by Garvey, government officials, FBI agents, lawyers, and dozens of others who were involved with the organization.

Jinx Coleman Broussard, *Giving a Voice to the Voiceless: Four Pioneering Black Women Journalists.* New York: Routledge, 2004. Biographical information about four women who fought for civil rights and women's equality during the twentieth century, including Amy Jacques Garvey, a strong leader within the UNIA and Marcus Garvey's second wife.

John Henrik Clarke, ed., *Marcus Garvey and the Vision of Africa.* New York: Random House, 1974. Essays by scholars, black leaders, and Marcus Garvey himself concerning the history of the UNIA and Garvey's life, his years of success, and the last years of his life.

Bettye Collier-Thomas and V.P. Franklin, eds., *Sisters in the Struggle.* New York: New York University Press, 2001. A collection of sixteen essays by African American women who actively participated in the civil rights and black power movements.

Elton C. Fax, *Garvey: The Story of a Pioneer Black Nationalist.* New York: Dodd, Mead, 1972. A study of Garvey based on source documents and interviews with UNIA members who were still alive when the book was written.

Milfred C. Fierce, *The Pan-African Idea in the United States, 1900–1919.* New York: Garland, 1993. A study of the early twentieth century movement that focused African American interest on returning to West Africa.

Amy Jacques Garvey, *Garvey and Garveyism.* New York: Octagon, 1978. A history of the man and the UNIA movement written by Marcus Garvey's second wife, who was also a leading Pan-Africanist and black nationalist leader who was the secretary-general of the UNIA for more than half a century.

Marcus Garvey, *Philosophy and Opinions of Marcus Garvey.* Ed. Amy Jacques Garvey. New York: Atheneum, 1980. The speeches, editorials, and articles of Marcus Garvey, first edited and published by his wife in 1923.

Imanuel Geiss, *The Pan-African Movement: A History of Pan-Africanism in America,*

Europe, and Africa. New York: Africana, 1974. Originally published in Germany in 1968, this book explores the Back to Africa movement from the early days of the slave trade through various incarnations in the nineteenth and twentieth centuries.

Robert A. Hill, ed., *Marcus Garvey, Life and Lessons: A Centennial Companion to the Marcus Garvey and Universal Negro Improvement Association Papers.* Berkeley and Los Angeles: University of California Press, 1987. A collection of autobiographical and philosophical works produced by Garvey from the time of his imprisonment in Atlanta to his death in 1940.

Theodore Kornweibel Jr., *Seeing Red: Federal Campaigns Against Black Militancy, 1919–1925.* Bloomington: Indiana University Press, 1998. A thoroughly documented account of government harassment, intimidation, surveillance, and arrest of African Americans and civil rights groups by J. Edgar Hoover and the Bureau of Investigation in the 1910s and 1920s.

Leon Litwack, *Trouble in Mind: Black Southerners in the Age of Jim Crow.* New York: Alfred A. Knopf, 1998. An exploration of the lives of black men and women during one of the most racially repressive eras in American history.

Alain Locke, ed., *The New Negro: An Interpretation.* New York: Arno, 1968. First published in 1925, this book, with its series of articles, essays, poems, and stories by black authors, brought worldwide attention to the literary movement of the Harlem Renaissance.

Tony Martin, *Race First: The Ideological and Organizational Struggles of Marcus Garvey and the Universal Negro Improvement Association.* Dover, MA: Majority, 1986. A thoroughly researched examination of the struggles, triumphs, and defeats of Marcus Garvey and the UNIA.

Wilson Jeremiah Moses, *Creative Conflict in African American Thought.* Cambridge, UK: Cambridge University Press, 2004. A book that analyzes the complexity of and contradictions in the philosophies of five major African American intellectuals, including Booker T. Washington, W.E.B. Du Bois, and Marcus Garvey.

Hugh Mulzac, *A Star to Steer By.* New York: International, 1963. The story of the UNIA steamship company, written by a captain on the Black Star Line.

Lens Nembhard, *Trials and Triumphs of Marcus Garvey.* Millwood, NY: Kraus Reprint, 1978. First published in Kingston in 1938, the author of this biography provides a Jamaican perspective to Garvey's life and politics in the 1920s and 1930s.

Roi Ottley, *New World A-Coming.* New York: Arno, 1968. First published in 1943, this book provides a picture of life in Harlem, through the eyes of the neighborhood's residents who describe how it feels to be black in a society dominated by white men.

Charles M. Payne and Adam Green, eds., *Time Longer than Rope: A Century of African American Activism.* New

York: New York University Press, 2003. An anthology of essays that detail the depth and breadth of black resistance and activism between 1850 and 1950.

Allan H. Spear, *Black Chicago: The Making of a Negro Ghetto, 1890–1920*. Chicago: University of Chicago Press, 1967. The history of a large black community during a crucial thirty-year period when a relatively positive system of race relations gave way to rigid segregation and discrimination.

Judith Stein, *The World of Marcus Garvey: Race and Class in Modern Society*. Baton Rouge: Louisiana State University Press, 1986. A comprehensive exploration of the life and times of Marcus Garvey with information about the Pan-African movement, ethnic politics, and the UNIA.

Ula Yvette Taylor, *The Veiled Garvey: The Life and Times of Amy Jacques Garvey*. Chapel Hill: University of North Carolina Press, 2002. A biography of Marcus Garvey's second wife, described by the author as "one of the most important, if largely unsung, Pan-African freedom fighters of the twentieth century."

Emory J. Tolbert, *The UNIA and Black Los Angeles: Ideology and Community in the American Garvey Movement*. Los Angeles: Center for Afro-American Studies, University of California, 1980.

Allen Weinstein and Frank Otto Gatell, eds., *The Segregation Era, 1863–1954: A Modern Reader*. New York: Oxford University Press, 1970. Essays about African American life, society, politics, and the struggle for equality in the era of segregation between the Emancipation Proclamation and the beginning modern civil rights movement.

Lionel M. Yard, *Biography of Amy Ashwood Garvey, 1897–1969: Co-Founder of the UNIA*. Washington, DC: Associated, 1990. A biography of UNIA cofounder, feminist, Pan-Africanist, and first wife of Marcus Garvey.

Periodicals

Amy Jacques Garvey, "Mrs. Amy Jacques Garvey Writes of Her Interesting Experiences," *Negro World*, November 17, 1923.

———, "Stop Hunting a Job and Create One," *Negro World*, October 9, 1926.

———, "Woman's Function in Life," *Negro World*, December 19, 1926.

———, "Women as Leaders Nationally and Racially," *Negro World*, October 24, 1925.

New York Age, "Old Fifteenth Given Rousing Reception," February 22, 1919. An article about the march through Harlem of the all-black 369th Infantry Regiment, formerly known as the Fifteenth Regiment of New York's National Guard.

Internet Sources

African Studies Center, "American Series Introduction: Volume I: 1826–August 1919," The Marcus Garvey and Universal Negro Improvement Association Papers Project, 2005. www.international.ucla.edu/africa/mgpp/.

Barbara Bair, "Online Forum: Comparing the Role of Women in the Garvey Movement," Public Broadcasting Service, 2000. www.pbs.org/wgbh/amex/garvey/sfeature/sf_forum_14.html.

Public Broadcasting Service, "People & Events: J. Edgar Hoover," 2000. www.pbs.org/wgbh/amex/garvey/peopleevents/p-hoover.html.

———, "The 'Garvey Must Go' Campaign," 2000. www.pbs.org/wgbh/amex/garvey/peopleevents/e_mustgo.html.

Index

Picture Credits

Cover, © CORBIS

© Bettmann/CORBIS, 12, 19, 22, 29 (both), 41, 42, 48, 62, 86, 89, 92

© David J. & Janice L. Frent Collection/CORBIS, 34

© Jacques M. Chenet/CORBIS, 96

© Hulton-Deutsch Collection/CORBIS, 47

© Underwood & Underwood/CORBIS, 38, 73-74

© CORBIS, 28

Hulton Archive by Getty Images, 16, 43, 83

Library of Congress, 25, 26, 32, 56, 68

National Portrait Gallery, 11

Courtesy of University of California Los Angeles, The Marcus Garvey Project, 50, 60, 76, 88

About the Author

Stuart A. Kallen is the author of more than two hundred nonfiction books for children and young adults. He has written on topics ranging from the theory of relativity to the history of rock and roll. In addition, Mr. Kallen has written award-winning children's videos and television scripts. In his spare time, Stuart A. Kallen is a singer/songwriter/guitarist in San Diego, California.